Basic Colour Photography

Andreas Feininger

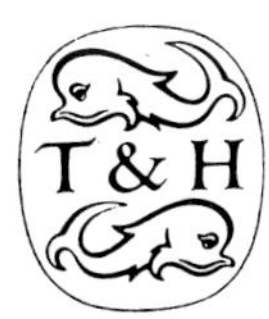

Thames and Hudson

Except for the pictures on p. 123, all photographs on pp. 53-127 were made in accordance with my instructions by

JOHN VELTRI,

whose talent and devotion to this venture contributed considerably to making this a better and more informative book than it would have been without his valuable help.

A. F.

First published in Great Britain in 1972 by Thames and Hudson Limited, London

Reprinted 1980

Produced in Singapore by
Graphic Consultants International Pte Ltd.

Table of Contents

A Clarification of Aims

Modern photo technology is so far advanced and foolproof that anyone who can read and follow simple instructions can also make *technically satisfactory photographs of average subjects* without the aid of this or any other photo guide as long as his equipment is suitable to the intended work. This is so because everything a beginner needs to know is already contained in the authoritative instructions that accompany every new camera, exposure meter, speedlight or other piece of photographic equipment, roll of film, or developing kit. Manufacturers of photographic supplies are fully aware that it is as much in their own interest as in that of the photographer that he use their products correctly and be satisfied with the results. Therefore, to reprint in a textbook information that is available free—a practice known as padding—seems to me not to be in the best interest of the reader, mainly because there simply are too many different kinds of cameras, exposure meters, films, developers, etc., to be specific—and when it comes to the technological aspects of photography, non-specific information is of very little help. Furthermore, because manufacturers continuously strive to improve their products, information pertaining to the operation of cameras, exposure meters, speedlights, the processing of films, etc., is easily outdated and may even be obsolete by the time a book appears in print. Experienced photographers know this and, instead of relying on books, get this kind of *short-lived information* in always authoritative form from the instruction sheets and booklets that accompany every new camera, roll or pack of film, developer, etc., as well as from photo magazines and the latest editions of the excellent, inexpensive Kodak Data Books, reference sources that I consider mandatory supplements to this or any other photo guide. It is for these reasons that certain "information" found in most other photo guides was not included in this text.

However, being able to make *technically satisfactory photographs of average subjects* is not the same as making *good* photographs, let alone "great" pictures—pictures that people remember. Such pictures are not so much the result of photo technical perfection (which any good photographer takes for granted but which can also be found in some of the most meaningless and boring pictures), as the result of a special way of seeing things.

Why? Because any subject can be "seen" and therefore photographed in a virtually unlimited number of different ways of which some, of course, are more effective than others. In other words, as a photographer, YOU HAVE A CHOICE. To teach you photography so that you will be able to take full advantage of this privilege of CHOICE was one of my main considerations in compiling this book.

This brings up the question of what is important and what superfluous when teaching a beginner "photography." Here, too, I have my own ideas, the outcome of 20 years of experience as a staff photographer for *Life*, one of the most exacting picture magazines in the world. Consequently, you will find in the following many things not found in ordinary photographic texts, but may miss certain subjects commonly taught in other guides like, for example, discussions on optics and how a lens produces a picture, or the composition of color films. In my opinion, such knowledge, interesting as it may be to specialists, contributes absolutely nothing to improving a photographer's work. Honestly—do you really believe that your pictures would have been better if you had known, for example, that any lens has seven basic faults called spherical and chromatic aberration, astigmatism, coma, etc., or that your color film consists of seven layers instead of five?

Likewise not found in this book will be what are popularly known as technical data—information pertaining to the make of camera and lens used to take a certain picture, *f*/stop, shutter speed, etc.—which are commonly printed in conjunction with the respective picture, allegedly as an aid to other photographers attempting a similar shot. In my experience, such data are not only valueless, but actually misleading because they are invariably incomplete and often fabricated. For example, what good are data on *f*/stop and shutter speed unless the brightness of the prevailing illumination is mentioned too (which it never is)? And what difference does it make whether a picture was taken, say, with a Leicaflex or a Pentax, with an *f*/1.4 instead of an *f*/1.8 or *f*/2 lens (which probably was stopped down anyway), whether it was made on Kodak or Agfa film? Not to mention that often the specific effect of a picture is due to, say, a fill-in light, or a particular filter, but neither one is mentioned in the data, either because of negligence on the part of the photographer or editor, or due to lack of space. Therefore, in the following, instead of being misled by spurious "data," the student photographer will be taught how to compile his own data—data to fit his particular requirements precisely.

In addition to solid technical instruction complemented by a series of photographs specifically taken for this book, the reader will find in the following a wealth of information on subjects which, although vitally important to the outcome of the picture, are rarely discussed in ordinary photo guides like, for example, how to choose the camera, lens, film, exposure meter, lighting equipment, etc., *most suitable to his particular kind of work*; the various controls in regard to light and lighting; control of contrast; the most effective use of color; how to avoid mistakes. For, although nothing is easier than to take snapshots of your family and friends and, a few days later, pick up at the store where you left your film a set of pretty pictures, few things require more expertise, patience, skill, and plain hard work than making photographs that leave a lasting impression. Because, in the last analysis, it is not technical perfection that makes a photograph memorable, but the intensity with which a photographer has experienced and the form in which he has expressed his subject. As in every art or craft, in photography, know-how is useless unless guided by know-why. To make sure that the reader learns not only the "how" but also the "why" of photography was another guiding principle in the compilation of this book.

ANDREAS FEININGER

I. The Means of Color Photography

If a photograph is good, credit must go to the photographer, not to the camera with which it was made. In itself, even the finest camera is no more creative than a lump of clay; but, like a lump of clay, in inspired hands, it can become a means of creation. With one provision: it must be suitable for the job.

Suitability of the photographic equipment is the number one prerequisite for success; the number two is simplicity. To give some examples: a $700 single-lens reflex camera, because it does not provide for perspective control, is bound to fail miserably if used for architectural photography, a field in which any $50 secondhand view camera is capable of producing outstanding results. For general photography, a relatively slow *f*/2 lens, because it is smaller, lighter, and probably sharper, is usually preferable to an *f*/1.4 high-speed lens, which may cost two or three times as much. And the photographer who is most loaded down with equipment is least likely to bring home good pictures because the complexity of his outfit will always get in his way, causing him to miss the most exciting shots.

For practicing photography on the first level—that of the beginner or the average photographer photographing average subjects—the means of photography are simple and, provided the camera is equipped with a built-in exposure meter, consist of only two items:

Camera (pp. 10–21)
Film (pp. 22–25)

For practicing photography on the second level—that of the advanced amateur, the professional, the specialist—one or more of the following additional pieces of equipment may be needed:

A second, different camera (pp. 10–21)
Additional interchangeable lenses (pp. 26–44)
A hand-held exposure meter (pp. 45–46)
Different filters and a polarizer (pp. 47–49)
Lighting equipment (pp. 50–54)
Extension bellows or reflex-housing (pp. 54–55)
Tripod or gunstock (p. 55)
Gadget bag (p. 55)

Photography on the first level

Although "first level" may smack of the beginner, perhaps 90 per cent of all the photographs taken by photographers all over the world belong in this category. Broadly speaking, it includes all average subjects photographed at average distances under average lighting conditions. In other words, without having to spend a lot of money on equipment, as long as his camera is suited to the job and he has film, a photographer can cover a surprisingly large amount of ground, including the following subjects:

People and portraits
Children and babies
Travel scenes
Landscapes
Street scenes
Domestic animals and pets

and, within certain limits:

Sports events
Theatre and stage

Photography on the second level

This is the domain of the creative amateur, the professional, the specialist, the imaginative experimenter. Suitably equipped—and in some cases the right equipment may cost several thousand dollars—photographers, by advancing to the second level, can expand the scope of their work enormously beyond that of the first level, including, among others, the following fields of photographic activity:

Aerial photography
Architectural photography
Close-up photography
Copying and reproduction
Experimental photography
Fashion photography
High-speed photography
Industrial photography
Infrared photography
Outdoor scenes at night
Photomicrography
Telephotography

HOW TO CHOOSE YOUR CAMERA

Entering a large photo store and scanning its displays with the intent of making up his mind which camera he should buy can be an almost traumatic experience for any photographic beginner—the choice seems overwhelming. There are small, medium, and large cameras, tiny ones and enormous ones; there are fairly cheap, medium priced, and terribly expensive cameras (Are they really worth their price in terms of usefulness and performance? Or are they primarily "status symbols"?); there are what look like the same kind of camera endlessly repeated in many models with different lenses differently priced—but what are their *real* differences as far as picture-making is concerned? How can an inexperienced beginner avoid making a costly mistake?

He can avoid making mistakes only if he approaches the purchase of a camera intelligently rather than emotionally, armed with facts instead of preconceived ideas, using his own judgment instead of falling for a salesman's softly persuasive chant. Specifically, he must begin by realizing that a camera—any camera—is basically nothing but a lighttight box, or sleeve, connecting two indispensible components:

the lens, which produces the picture (pp. 26–44),
the film, which retains it (pp. 22–25).

Its other controls and appendages are merely auxiliary devices, the purpose of which is to enable a photographer to perform the three operations required to make a picture:

Aiming (p. 56)
Focusing (p. 58)
Exposing (p. 67)

And as far as learning how to operate your newly acquired treasure is concerned, do not worry: authoritative and complete instructions for use accompany every new camera (or, for that matter, almost any other piece of photographic equipment). Thorough study of these instructions augmented by extensive practicing is the best and fastest way of learning how to make the most of your camera's inherent potential.

It cannot be overemphasized that the first prerequisite for success in photography is a camera that is suited for the job for which it will be used. In my experience, the greatest mistake a photographer can make is, instead of selecting his camera on the basis of its suitability, to select it on the basis of prestige, popularity, or advertising pressure, or buying the most expensive camera he can afford on the assumption that it must also be the best or one publicized by a famous photographer whose work he admires, heedless of whether or not it suits his own personality and type of work. This is a sure invitation to disaster. It can only be avoided if the photographer chooses his camera under careful consideration of the three main characteristics of any camera:

Design (pp. 11–15)
Film size (pp. 16–19)
Quality (p. 19)

In regard to DESIGN

Cameras can be classified as belonging to 1 of 2 main groups and 11 subgroups:

General-purpose cameras:

Box and simple roll-film cameras
Single-lens reflex cameras
Twin-lens reflex cameras
Rangefinder 35mm cameras
Press-type cameras

More or less specialized cameras:

View cameras
Super wide-angle cameras
Aerial cameras
Polaroid Land cameras
Panoramic cameras
Subminiature cameras

Each of these camera designs has specific qualities that make it particularly well suited to certain types of photographic work and more or less unsuited to anything else. These are discussed in the following survey.

General-purpose cameras

These are designed for hand-held operation but can, of course, also be used on a tripod. They are primarily intended for photographing average subjects under average conditions. Most of the better ones feature interchangeability of lenses and are therefore suitable to wide-angle and telephotography. Many are partly and a few are fully automated, reducing correct exposure to the lining up of a pointer and a slot, or performing this operation completely automatically.

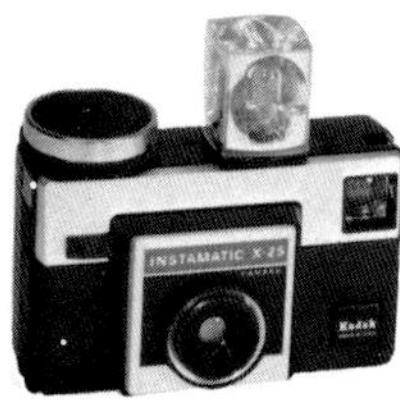

Box and simple roll-film cameras are little more than toys designed to fill the needs of the occasional snapshooter who wishes to take pictures with a minimum expenditure of cash, mental effort, and technical know-how. Their potential is, of course, extremely limited.

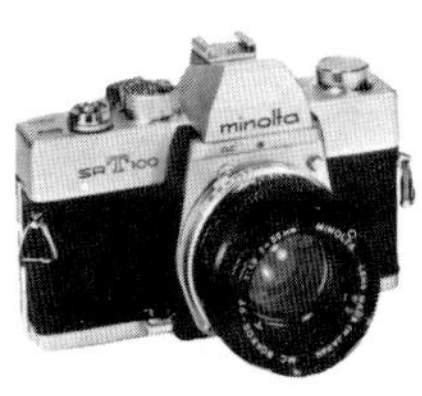

Single-lens reflex cameras represent the most adaptable and therefore generally most useful (and popular) camera design but are relatively complex and more subject to malfunction than any other camera type. They are particularly suitable for photographing dynamic subjects, such as people and action, and for wide-angle and telephotography. Since they are completely free of parallax (discrepancy between the image as seen in the viewfinder and as rendered on the film), they are ideal for close-up photography (if necessary, in conjunction with extension tubes or auxiliary bellows). And they represent the only camera design that permits the use of zoom lenses (p. 44).

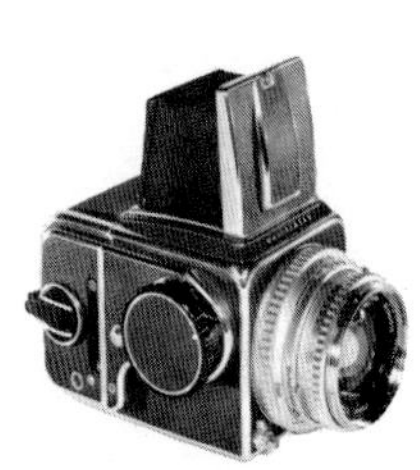

SLR's (as they are often called for short) come in two main sizes designed for 35mm and 120 roll film (pp. 16–17), respectively. The first, which is normally held at eye-level, is best for color slides (the worldwide standard is 35mm) and fast shooting as in documentary work; the second, which is normally held at waist level, is recommended to photographers who insist on highest print quality if working in black and white, or prefer color paper prints to color slides.

Twin-lens reflex cameras (TLR's for short), in comparison with SLR's, have several advantages: the finder

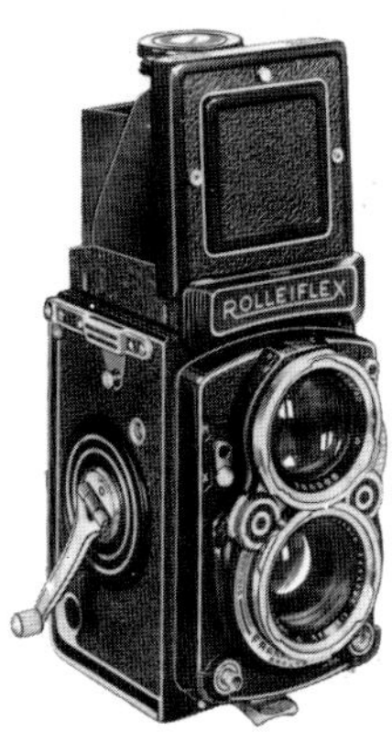

image stays bright no matter how much the taking lens is stopped down and is continually visible, even during exposure; operation is very quiet and completely vibration free; regular (instead of special FP) flashbulbs can be used, and electronic flash can be synchronized at any shutter speed. Drawbacks: Most TLR's don't provide for lens interchangeability and cannot be used for wide-angle or telephotography, nor are they suitable for the more extreme kind of close-ups. The extent of sharpness in depth (p. 62) cannot be checked visually.

TLR's are particularly suitable for general photography and ideal for beginners.

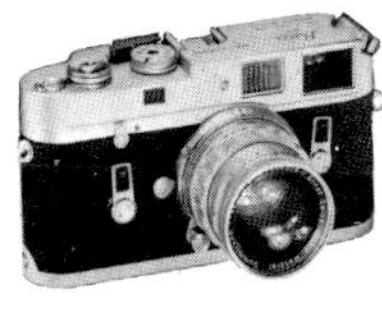

Rangefinder cameras (RF's for short), in 35mm size, are preferentially used by many of the most successful photojournalists and, in 4″ × 5″ size, by large numbers of press photographers. RF's are particularly fast in operation and well suited to wide-angle and *moderate* telephotography, but 35mm RF's require a special reflex-housing before they can be used for close-ups and more extreme telephotography. Lens interchangeability is normally provided.

Drawbacks: Smallness of finder image; no visual check for sharpness in depth; no built-in exposure meter; restriction to the lenses provided by the camera manufacturer; rangefinder may go "out of sync" without the photographer noticing it until it is too late (see test described on p. 35).

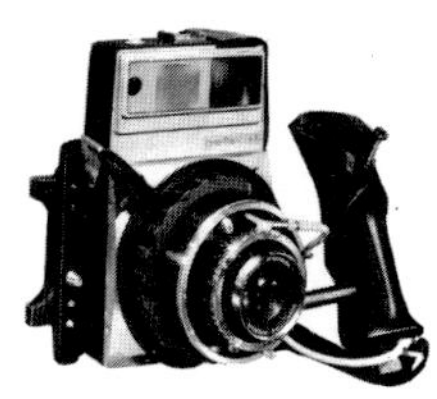

Press-type cameras (the standard used to be the 4″ × 5″ Speed Graphic) are large RF cameras designed originally for use with sheet film. They are gradually being replaced by more modern designs built to take 120 and 220 roll film, of which the Koni-Omega, Linhof Press 70 and Model 220, and Graflex XL are typical. These cameras are particularly suitable for general photography in cases in which the photographer insists on higher print quality than attainable with 35mm film. The most popular film size is 2¼″ × 2¾″, the so-called "ideal format" because it permits the photographer to make 8″ × 10″ or 11″ × 14″ enlargements without wasting any part of the film.

More or less specialized cameras

Such cameras are particularly well suited to some types of photographic work but, because of certain design characteristics, are not particularly suited, and may even be totally unfit, for others. None of the types described below is suitable for general photography, and anyone considering buying one should be aware of its applications and limitations. These are the "second cameras" that ambitious photographers acquire to get an advantage over their less enterprising competitors.

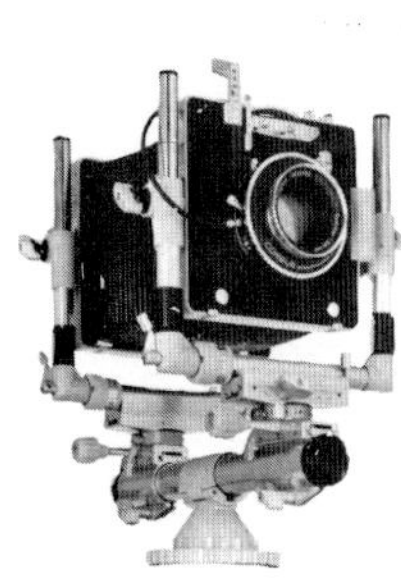

View cameras, because they lack viewfinders, cannot be used hand-held but must be placed on a tripod. As a result, though unsurpassed for photographing static subjects, they are totally useless for dynamic ones. They should be the first choice of anyone specializing in architectural, industrial, interior, or commercial product photography, or in making reproductions of works of art. They can be equipped with any type and make of lens, as long as it is mounted in a shutter, and are equally suited to wide-angle, telephoto, and close-up photography. They have, furthermore, the only camera design that can (and usually is) equipped with individually adjustable front and back movements (the so-called "swings") for perspective control.

The most advanced view cameras are constructed according to the module (or building-block) principle with virtually all their components—bellows, front and rear standard, track, lens shade, etc.—detachable and interchangeable with other parts of similar function but of different size or design in accordance with different photographic requirements. Consequently, a photographer can not only custom tailor his view camera to fit his purpose exactly but, if necessary, can later expand it to fit any other task (or film size!) as well. Standard is 4″ × 5″ sheet film, but models in smaller or larger sizes are available too, and all can be fitted with roll-film adapters.

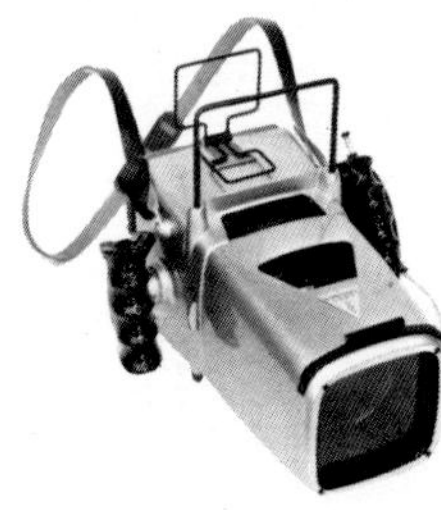

Aerial cameras, because their lenses are permanently focused at infinity, are unsurpassed for aerial photography and useless for any other purpose. In particular, photographers should beware of buying one of the so-called "surplus" aerial cameras often advertised at fantastically low prices in the hope of converting it to other uses; it simply cannot be done at a reasonable cost.

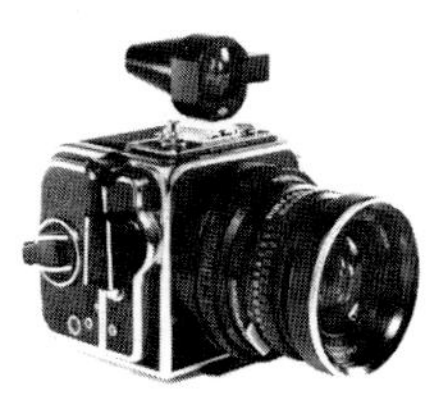

Super-wide-angle cameras, which encompass angles of view that range from 90° to 180° depending on the respective design and lens, are suitable only for extreme wide-angle photography or the creation of the typical wide-angle perspective characterized by extreme "distortion." Typical representatives available at the time of writing are the Hasselblad Superwide 2¼″ × 2¼″, the Plaubel Veriwide 2¼″ × 3¼″, and a number of 35mm cameras equipped with 180° fish-eye and other extreme wide-angle lenses (p. 41).

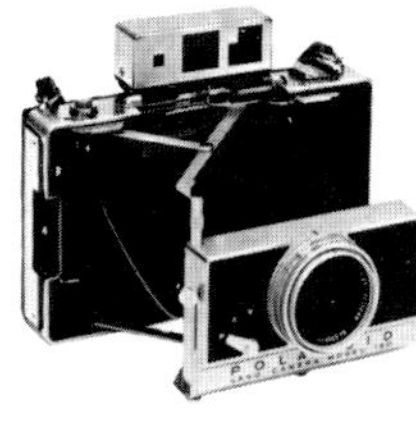

Polaroid Land cameras—the well-known "picture-in-a-minute" cameras—are specialized insofar as they can be used only in conjunction with Polaroid Land films, most of which don't yield a useable negative. They are valued by amateurs for obvious reasons and by professionals for making on-the-spot exposure checks and for producing instant giveaway pictures as rewards for cooperation. Special Polaroid Land backs are also available for use in conjunction with ordinary 4″ × 5″ and a few other cameras.

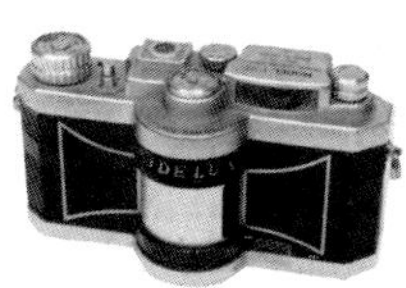

Panoramic cameras are equipped with wide-angle lenses that describe an arc during exposure. They are extreme wide-angle cameras with angles of view of approximately 140° which produce pictures in cylindrical perspective, *i.e.*, all straight lines not parallel with the axis of the "swing" are rendered curved, increasingly so, the closer they are to the edges of the picture. This unusual perspective manifests itself, of course, only if the subject contains straight lines and usually makes panoramic cameras unsuitable to architectural photography, but is unnoticeable in ordinary outdoor scenes.

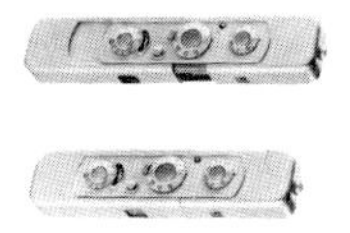

Subminiature cameras are often precision instruments equipped with the most sophisticated refinements. In my opinion, they are invaluable in cases in which smallness is of the essence but useless in all others.

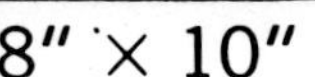

Standard color film sizes

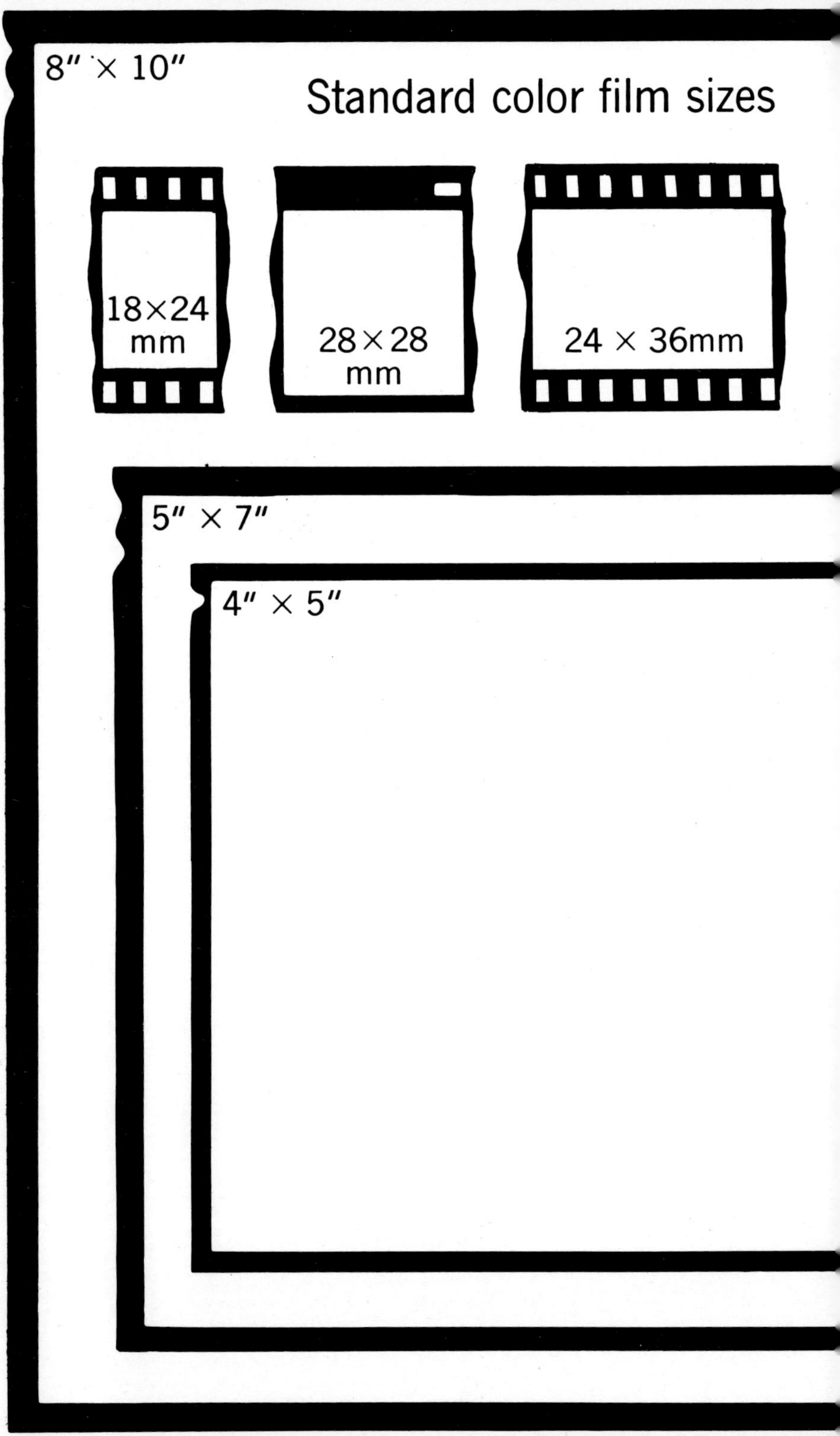

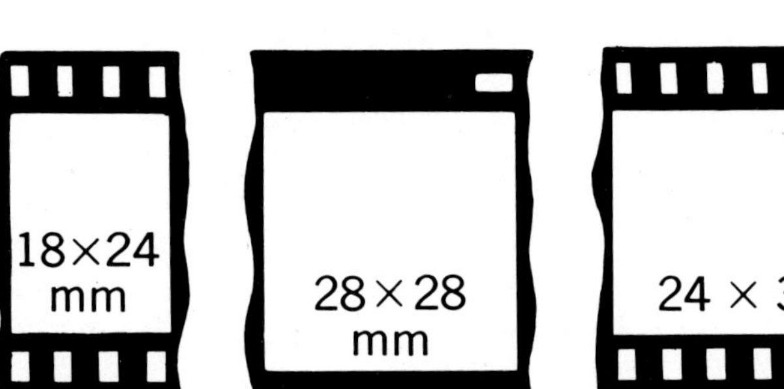

5″ × 7″

4″ × 5″

The six smaller formats are available only in the form of roll film, the three larger ones only in the form of sheet film. All are shown here in their actual size.

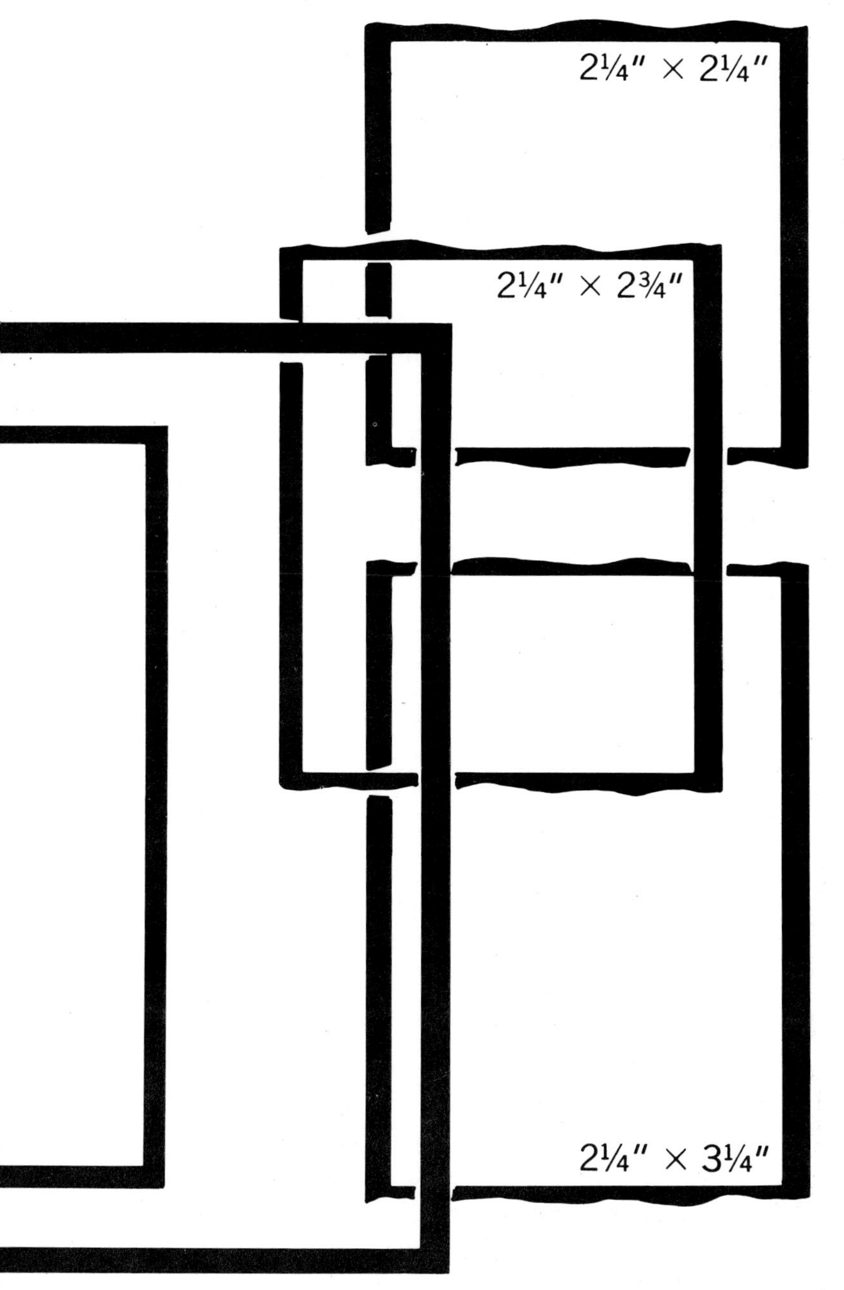

In regard to FILM SIZE

Cameras can be classified as belonging to one of the following four categories, each of which has specific advantages and drawbacks:

1. Single-frame (sometimes called half-frame) 18 × 24mm and smaller (subminiature) cameras are invaluable in cases in which smallness and portability are the prime requirements (as in spying). In all other cases, their performance will be disappointing due to the relatively low technical quality of the transparencies and prints that they yield. This is the inevitable result of the fact that small film sizes, in order to produce effective pictures, must be enlarged more times than larger ones, a process that reduces sharpness and accentuates the film grain in direct proportion to the scale of the enlargement.

2. 35mm cameras (negative size 24 × 36mm) represent a compromise between portability (the smaller, the better) and picture quality (the larger, the better). They are capable of yielding very satisfactory results *provided the photographer is a clean and careful worker,* although a stickler for print quality will probably be disappointed and is advised to work with a larger film size. In addition to smallness and convenience, 35mm cameras offer the following advantages over cameras of larger size: inconspicuousness; availability of lenses of much higher speed than for large cameras; film for 100 exposures takes less space than a pack of cigarettes; high speed of operation and low cost per exposure combine to make for a more thorough coverage of the subject. All this plus the fact that 35mm film is the worldwide standard for color slides combine to make the 35mm camera today's most popular camera type and the one best suited for photographing dynamic subjects—people, action, animals.

Drawbacks are inferior sharpness and tonal quality of the enlarged picture; temptation to overshoot and waste film on inconsequential subjects; necessity for more critical processing; and very low sales appeal of the small color transparencies.

3. Cameras designed to take 120 or 220 roll film come in two main sizes, yielding negatives 2¼″ × 2¼″ and 2¼″ × 2¾″ large, respectively. The latter size, the so-called "ideal format," has virtually the same proportions as an 8″ × 10″ or 11″ × 14″ print, making it possible to enlarge the entire negative without any loss through cropping.

In my opinion, cameras designed to take 120 or 220 roll film come as close to the all-purpose ideal as possible, representing the best compromise between portability on one side and picture quality on the other. They are particularly recommended to photographers who are equally interested in dynamic and static subjects—people as well as things—and to those who prefer color paper prints to color slides.

4. Cameras designed for use with large films (sheet film) come in three main sizes: 4″ × 5″, 5″ × 7″, and 8″ × 10″, of which 4″ × 5″ is the standard large camera format. In comparison with smaller formats, large negatives and transparencies have the advantage of superior apparent sharpness and tonal gradation at any given print size and hence much greater sales appeal, which is particularly evident in regard to color prints and transparencies. The main drawbacks of large cameras are slowness of operation, high cost per exposure, bulkiness and weight of the outfit, and the fact that view cameras can only be used mounted on a tripod.

A large camera should be the first choice of the photographer who specializes in static subjects and the perfectionist who is willing to accept certain inconveniences in the interest of the highest technical print and color quality.

In regard to QUALITY

Distinguish between precision cameras made primarily for professional use, cameras of average workmanship intended for the average amateur, and cameras of low quality designed for the occasional weekend snapshooter. Quality, of course, is directly related to price. And since a precision camera invariably is better designed and made of better material, longer lasting, and especially more reliable than a camera of lower quality, it is my opinion that, as a rule, it is more advantageous to apply a given sum of money to the purchase of a *secondhand precision camera* or a *discontinued top-quality model* than to spend the same amount on a brand-new, latest-model camera of inherently lower quality, provided, of course, that one deals with a reputable camera store that guarantees its merchandise.

Summary relating camera purpose and design

The first list contains in alphabetical order 22 different fields of photographic activity, each followed by a row of numbers, each number representing one of the 17 different camera qualities listed in the second list. By correlating these two lists, anyone should be able to find quickly the kind of camera that is best suited to his purpose.

Advertising (live models) 2, 5, 9
Advertising (product photography) 3, 5, 11, 12, 15
Animals (domestic and pets) 2, 9
Animals (wildlife) 1, 5, 7, (14, 16), 17
Architecture 3, 5, 6, 11, 15
Children and babies 1 or 2, 9
Close-up photography 1 or 2 or 3, 5, 9, 10, 12
Copying and reproductions 1 or 3, 10, 12, 15
Fashion photography 2, (4), 5, 9
Food photography 3, 5, 10, 11, 12, 15
General photography 1 or 2, 5, 9, 17
Industrial photography 5, 6, 9, 11, 12, 15, (16)
Interiors 3, 5, 6, 9, 11, 15
Landscapes 3, 5, 15, 17
Nature photography (general) 1 or 2, 5, 9, 10, 12, 17
News, documentary photography 1, 4, 5, (7), 9, 13, (16), 17
Objects and works of art 3, 5, 10, 11, 12, 15
People (general) 1 or 2, 5, 9, 13, 14, (16), 17
Portraiture 1 or 2 or 3, 5, 9
Sports photography 1 or 2, 5, (6, 7), 8, 9, 13, 16, 17
Theater and stage 1 or 2, 4, 5, 9, 14
Travel photography 1 or 2, 4, 5, 9, 14, 17

1. **Small cameras** designed for 35mm film.
2. **Medium-sized cameras** yielding $2\frac{1}{4}'' \times 2\frac{1}{4}''$ or $2\frac{1}{4}'' \times 2\frac{3}{4}''$ negatives.
3. **Large cameras** designed for $4'' \times 5''$ or larger sheet film.
4. **Lens speed:** the fastest lenses are made for 35mm cameras only.
5. **Provision for lens interchangeability.**

6. **Extreme wide-angle lenses:** 180° fish-eye lenses are available only for 35mm SLR's, but special accessory lenses can convert most standard lenses into 180° fish-eye lenses. For specific wide-angle cameras see p. 13. The Goerz Hypergon lenses cover 130° in conjunction with special boxlike $5'' \times 7''$ or $8'' \times 10''$ view-type cameras.

7. **Extreme telephoto lenses** are available only for 35mm SLR and RF and 2¼″ × 2¼″ SLR cameras; 35mm RF cameras require the use of a special reflex-housing.

8. **Shutter speed:** focal-plane shutters can provide speeds of up to 1/2000 sec., between-the-lens shutters up to 1/800 sec.

9. **Flash synchronization:** between-the-lens shutters can be synchronized with any kind of flash at any shutter speed; focal-plane shutters require special FP flashbulbs, synchronize with electronic flash only at relatively slow shutter speeds.

10. **Freedom from parallax** (see p. 12): SLR's and view cameras are free of parallax; a reflex-housing transforms a 35mm RF camera into a parallax-free SLR. RF's and TLR's are subject to parallax and require special parallax-compensating devices.

11. **Perspective control:** only swing-equipped view cameras provide for full control; swing-equipped press-type cameras and 35mm SLR's equipped with the Nikkor PC or Schneider PA-Curtagon lenses allow a limited degree of perspective control.

12. **Extended extension** between lens and film: extra-long bellows (double or triple extension) are provided by certain view and press-type cameras; extension rings or tubes or auxiliary bellows can be used in conjunction with all 35mm and 2¼″ × 2¼″ cameras featuring interchangeability of lenses.

13. **Speed of operation:** RF's are fastest, closely followed by 35mm SLR's with built-in exposure meter and automatic diaphragm; 2¼″ × 2¼″ SLR's are somewhat slower.

14. **Noise level:** between-the-lens shutters are quieter than focal-plane shutters. RF's are quieter than SLR's. Loudest are certain 2¼″ × 2¼″ SLR's.

15. **Sharpness of rendition:** potentially, 4″ × 5″ and larger cameras are capable of producing sharper pictures with better tonal and color gradation than smaller cameras.

16. **Sequence-shooting:** a few 35mm and 2¼″ × 2¼″ cameras either have or can be equipped with battery- or spring-driven motors for rapid-sequence "firing."

17. **Size and weight:** considerable differences exist between cameras that produce negatives or transparencies of the same size. Generally, RF's are lighter and less bulky than SLR's, which in turn are lighter and less bulky than TLR's.

HOW TO CHOOSE YOUR FILM

To find the film best suited to your particular kind of work, consider the following aspects:

Size

Obviously, the film has to fit the camera in which it is to be used. However, photographers contemplating the purchase of a new camera (and those using cameras that by means of adapters or inserts accommodate different sizes of film) should weigh the advantages and drawbacks of small, medium, and large film sizes, which I discussed on pp. 16–19, before finalizing their choice.

Roll film and 35mm film permit fastest camera operation, are the most compact form of film, and represent the most convenient type insofar as they may be loaded into, and taken out of, the camera even in full daylight (although never in direct sunlight; if there is no shadow, turn away from the sun and load the camera in the shadow of your body). Drawbacks are: unless he is prepared to sacrifice unexposed film, a photographer can develop his film and see the results only after the last frame on the roll has been exposed; impossibility of changing from one film type to another, or from color to black and white, before the entire roll is exposed (unless the camera permits the use of dark slide-equipped, interchangeable film magazines); except for roll film designed for use in aerial cameras, the largest available size is 2¼″ × 3¼″.

Sheet film (standard size is 4″ × 5″) enables a photographer to develop individual shots individually and to switch from one type of color film to another (or to black and white) at any time without sacrificing unexposed film. Drawbacks are that each sheet of film must be loaded individually into the holder in total darkness; that two sheets of 4″ × 5″ film in their holder take as much space and weigh approximately as much as 35mm film for more than 100 shots; and that, as far as operating a camera is concerned it is the slowest type of film. Sheet film is available in sizes from 2¼″ × 3¼″ up to 8″ × 10″ and larger.

Speed

The measure of a film's light sensitivity, or "speed," is its ASA number; the higher the ASA number, the faster the film and, other factors being equal, the shorter the required exposure, or the smaller the required diaphragm stop with corresponding increase in the extent of the sharply covered zone in depth (pp. 62–63). In this respect, ASA 25 represents a slow, ASA 160 a medium-fast, and ASA 400 a high-speed color film.

Negative color films

These yield color negatives, *i.e.*, the colors of the subject appear in their complementary shades (red, for example, appears as green, yellow as blue). Like ordinary black-and-white negatives, such color negatives must be printed before they yield useable pictures. In comparison with positive color films (p. 24), negative color films have the following advantages:

Because a color negative is only the interim stage of a more complex process, a color photographer has as much control over the appearance of his picture as the man who works in black and white (see also pp. 116–117). In particular, he can correct a considerable degree of overexposure and a somewhat lesser degree of underexposure and thereby eliminate the need for "bracketing" (p. 73); he can improve unsatisfactory color rendition, on the overall as well as on the local scale; and he can, if necessary, increase or decrease, respectively, the contrast of his picture. Other advantages are that the valuable, unique negatives can be kept by the photographer who sends out only "expendable" prints; that a single negative can yield any number of "original" paper prints; and that small-sized cameras can be made to yield large-sized color prints.

Drawbacks are the impossibility of "editing" from color negatives, which must be contact printed before they can be evaluated by the photographer; the comparatively long time interval between shooting the picture and seeing the final result; the print contrast, brilliance, and color saturation are inferior to those of projected color slides; the relatively high cost per finished print.

Negative color films are intended for use with daylight or electronic flash. If used in conjunction with tungsten lamps or photofloods, the appropriate color-conversion filter must be used and the film speed reduced in accordance with the instructions that accompany the film.

Positive (reversal) color films

Such films yield positive color transparencies (slides) suitable for viewing, projection, and reproduction by photomechanical means. They are, at least at the present time, less suited for making color prints on paper, a process that normally requires the making of an internegative (color negative). In comparison with negative color films, positive color films have the following advantages:

Lower cost per picture because the developed film is already the final product and no printing is required, a characteristic that has the further advantage that it cuts down the time interval between shooting the picture and seeing (and editing) the final result—a bonus to many professional photographers; superior color brilliance, sharpness, and definition.

Drawbacks are that, since it is virtually impossible to correct mistakes once the film has been exposed, unless light conditions and exposure are perfect, the transparency will be disappointing; and that every transparency is an original and as such unique, and if damaged or lost, is gone forever. It is, of course, possible to duplicate a color transparency, but this is a fairly complicated, costly, and time-consuming process involving "masking" if the duplicate should match the original. To avoid such possibilities, experienced color photographers make it a rule always to shoot several exposures of any important subject, merely to provide themselves with some "spares."

Positive color films are made in the following three types, each of which is intended for use ("balanced") with a specific type of light. Unless the right type of film is used in conjunction with the right type of light (or the appropriate color-conversion filter is used), the color of the transparency will not match the color of the subject, and the effect will be "unnatural."

Daylight-type color film is intended for use with standard daylight (a combination of direct sunlight and light reflected from a clear blue sky with a few white clouds during the hours when the sun is more than 20° above the horizon) or with electronic flash.

Type A color film is intended for use with amateur photoflood lamps with a color temperature (p. 86) of 3400 K.

Type B color film is intended for use with professional tungsten lamps with a color temperature of 3200 K.

GENERAL ADVICE ON HANDLING FILM

When buying film, check the expiration date that is stamped on the wrapping; it is your guarantee of freshness. Outdated film may be partly or wholly fogged, or may have lost some of its speed or contrast, or may yield unsatisfactory colors.

Never load or unload your camera in bright light or your film may be light-struck; if there is no shade, turn away from the sun and work in the shadow cast by your body.

When loading roll film, carefully thread the end of the paper into the slot of the takeup spool, fold it over sharply, and make sure that it does not form a bulge; if it does, your film may become light-struck.

When loading sheet film into holders, make sure that the emulsion side faces the slide. The emulsion side faces you if the notches that identify the film type are in the upper righthand corner while the film is held vertically.

Do not touch the film emulsion with your fingers (for example, when loading sheet film in the darkroom), for the always present sweat droplets would leave indelible marks, or "fingerprints." When handling transparencies, hold them only by the edges.

Dampness and heat are the worst enemies of unexposed film and slowly destroy negatives and transparencies. Therefore, film, no matter whether unexposed, exposed but not yet developed, or developed, must be stored in a dry and cool place. Unexposed film in the original (unopened) wrapping is best stored in a freezer but must be given several hours to thaw before it can be used.

On cold, dry days, move the film transport lever and rewind crank of your camera slowly; otherwise friction-generated static electricity may leave nasty marks in the form of stars or wriggly lines on the film.

Don't forget to rewind 35mm film into the magazine before opening the camera back.

To avoid gradual deterioration of the latent image, exposed film should be developed as soon as possible.

HOW TO CHOOSE YOUR LENS

Although most cameras are sold complete with lens (exception: view cameras, where the lens is always sold separately), the fact that most cameras are also offered with a variety of different lenses from which the prospective buyer must choose, plus the fact that many cameras permit interchanging the original lens with a variety of other lenses with different characteristics, makes it imperative that the student photographer be sufficiently familiar with the basic qualities and types of lenses so that he can make an intelligent choice. For, next to choosing the most suitable type of camera and film, selection of the most suitable kind of lens is a prerequisite for success. Knowledgeable photographers choose their lenses on the basis of three factors:

Lens characteristics (pp. 26–33)
Lens performance (pp. 34–39)
Lens type (pp. 40–44)

Lens CHARACTERISTICS

Regardless of performance and type, a lens has three main characteristics that determine what it can and cannot do:

Focal length (pp. 26–28)
Relative aperture or "speed" (pp. 28–31)
Covering power (p. 32)

Focal length is that quality of a lens which determines the size of the image on the film (the scale of rendition). Focal length and image size are directly proportional: the longer the focal length, the larger the scale of rendition—a lens with a focal length twice as long as that of another lens renders the subject twice as high and wide on the film. Consequently, if a photographer wishes to show his subject in larger scale without moving closer to it (which is often impractical, impossible, or undesirable and, furthermore, always involves a change in perspective), he must take the picture with a lens of longer focal length—one of the reasons why so many cameras provide for interchangeability of lenses.

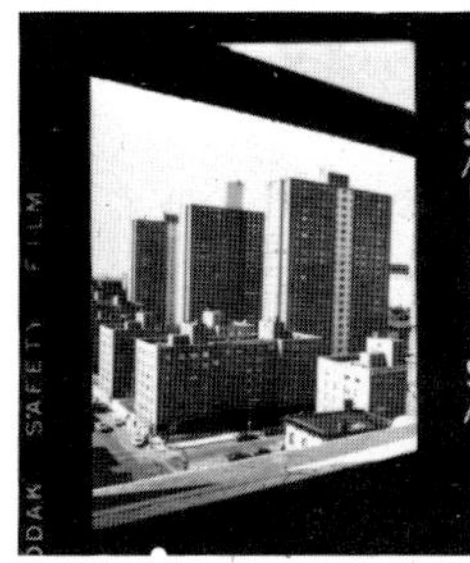

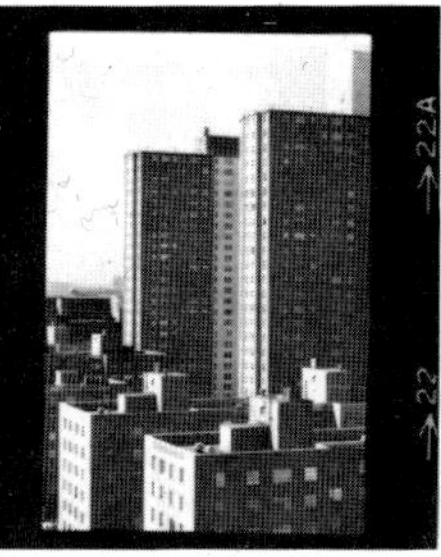

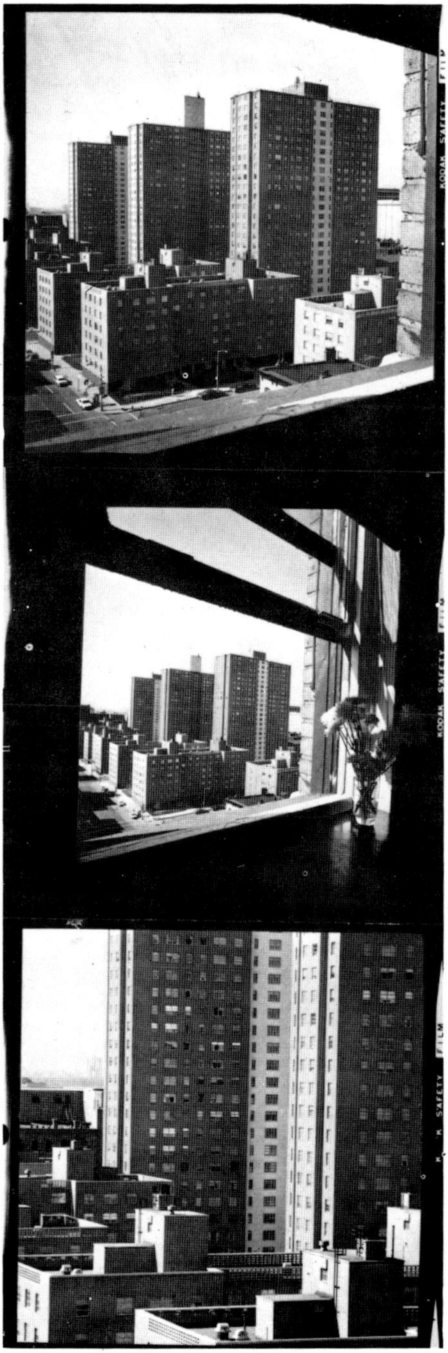

Focal length, scale, and angle of view

Top left: pair of pictures taken on 35mm film with a standard lens (left) and a moderate telephoto lens (right), respectively. The strip at the right was taken with a 2¼" × 2¼" camera with a standard, a wide-angle, and a telephoto lens, respectively.

The wide-angle lens, having a shorter focal length than either the standard or the telephoto lens, shows the subject in smaller scale but includes a wider angle of view. Conversely, the telephoto lens, having a longer focal length than either the standard or the wide-angle lens, shows the subject in larger scale but includes a correspondingly narrower angle of view.

Note that, despite the difference in angle of view, the scale of rendition of the 35mm telephotograph is identical to that of the 2¼" × 2¼" shot made with the lens of standard focal length. Why? Because both were taken from the same camera position *with lenses of identical focal lengths*, in this case, 80mm.

The focal length of a lens is normally engraved on its mount and given either in inches, centimeters, or millimeters. It designates the distance between approximately the center of the lens* and the film at which the lens produces a sharp picture of an object located infinitely far away, for example, a star. In this position—the shortest lens-to-film distance at which a lens can produce a sharp image—the lens is said to be focused at infinity.

Popularly, lenses are often referred to as standard, long-focus, or short-focus lenses. This classification is, of course, meaningful only in reference to a specific film format: in conjunction with, say, a 2¼″ × 2¼″ camera, which has a standard lens with a focal length of 3 or 3⅛ inches, a lens with a focal length of 8 inches is obviously a long-focus lens, but used on an 8″ × 10″ view camera (standard lens: 14-inch focal length), it just as obviously would have to be considered a short-focus lens. Popularly, the term long-focus lens is often equated with telephoto lens, the term short-focus lens with wide-angle lens. A standard lens always has a focal length equal to, or only *slightly* longer or shorter than, the diagonal of the film size in conjunction with which it is to be used. In comparison with a long-focus (telephoto) or a short-focus (wide-angle) lens, as far as the perspective of the picture is concerned, a standard lens produces a more "natural-appearing" rendition (provided the scale of rendition of the respective pictures is the same). This is the main reason why the first lens that a photographer acquires if he buys a camera with interchangeable lenses should always be a lens of standard focal length.

Relative aperture, or "speed," is that quality of a lens which determines its maximum light transmission. In this respect, other factors being equal, a "fast" or "high-speed" lens has two advantages over a "slower" one: it permits a photographer to use a higher shutter speed (and thereby to "stop" subject motion or avoid accidental camera movement during exposure more effectively, which would cause blur); and it enables him to keep the sharply covered zone in depth more shallow and thereby heighten the feeling of "depth" in his picture. Therefore, potentially, a fast lens offers a creative photographer more scope than a slower lens, although it may also have certain drawbacks (p. 40).

*Specifically, the so-called "node of emission," which normally lies slightly behind the center of the lens. In telephoto and retrofocus wide-angle lenses, the node of emission lies outside the lens.

Focal length

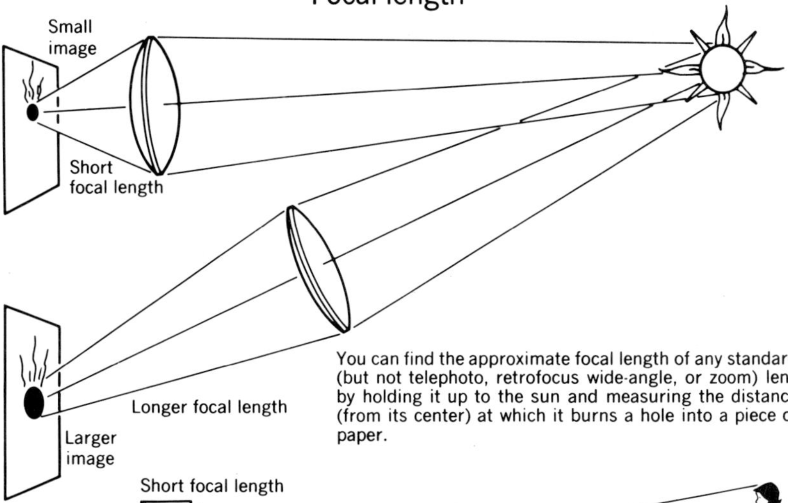

Small image

Short focal length

Longer focal length

Larger image

You can find the approximate focal length of any standard (but not telephoto, retrofocus wide-angle, or zoom) lens by holding it up to the sun and measuring the distance (from its center) at which it burns a hole into a piece of paper.

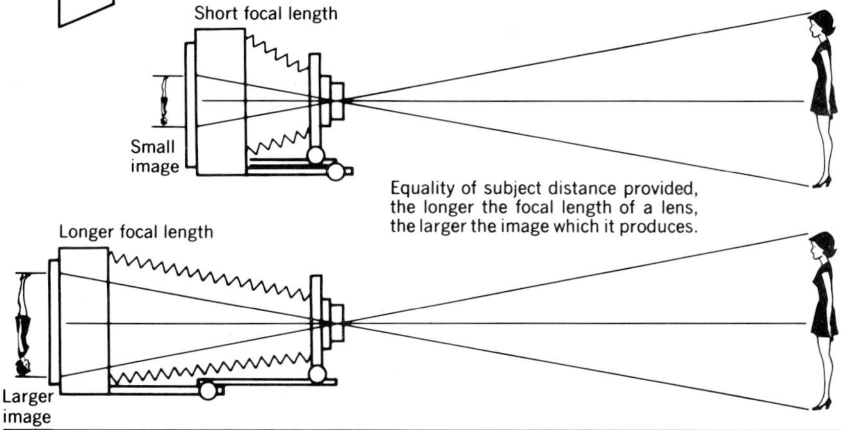

Short focal length

Small image

Equality of subject distance provided, the longer the focal length of a lens, the larger the image which it produces.

Longer focal length

Larger image

Relative aperture

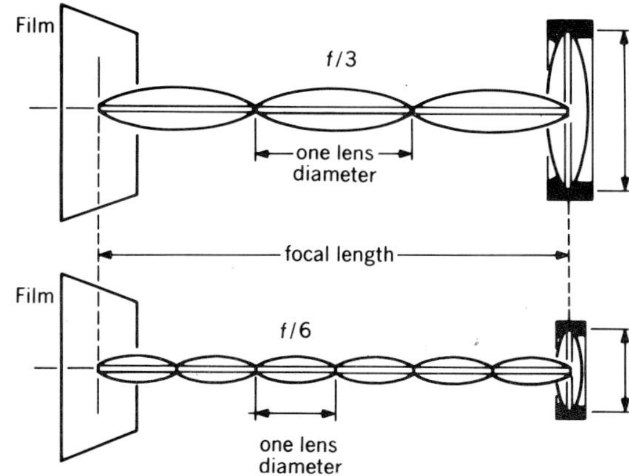

Schematical drawing of two lenses of equal focal length (producing images of equal sizes) but different relative apertures and therefore different "speeds"; see explanation on p. 30.

The relative aperture of a lens, which is usually engraved on the lens mount, is always expressed in the form of a ratio: focal length (f) divided by effective lens diameter. For example, a standard lens for a 4″ × 5″ camera has a focal length of 6 inches; if such a lens has an effective diameter of, say, 1¼ inches, its relative aperture would be 6:1¼ = 4.8 and expressed in the familiar form *f*/4.8. If, on the other hand, a lens of 6 inches focal length has an effective diameter of, say, 1¾ inches, its relative aperture would be 6:1¾ = 3.4 and expressed as *f*/3.4.

Now, it is obvious that the lens with the larger diameter transmits more light and hence has a higher "speed" than the lens with the smaller diameter. It is less obvious—particularly to the beginner—that the lens that has the *higher* speed should be denoted by the *lower* *f*/number, although the foregoing explanation should clarify this apparent paradox. In this respect, *f*/1.4 and *f*/1.8 typify high-speed lenses, *f*/2.8 and *f*/3.5 lenses of medium speed, and *f*/6.3 or *f*/9 relatively slow lenses.

In practice, for reasons that have to do with correct exposure and the extent of sharpness in depth (pp. 63 and 69), a lens will rarely be used at its maximum aperture. Usually, it is necessary to reduce its aperture to a greater or lesser extent, an operation that is performed with the aid of the *diaphragm,* a variable aperture built into the lens; this operation is called "stopping down the lens."

So that a photographer may know precisely how far his lens is stopped down (a prerequisite for correct exposure), the diaphragm is calibrated in *f*/numbers, or "*f*/stops," in such a way that reducing the aperture by one *f*/stop number requires doubling the exposure time, and increasing the aperture by one *f*/stop number requires halving the exposure time, if the result should be the same in terms of color rendition of the transparency or density of the negative. To give an example: in bright sunlight, a film with a speed (p. 23) of ASA 160 would be correctly exposed if the diaphragm is set at *f*/12.5 and the shutter at 1/200 sec. However, as far as color rendition or negative density are concerned, the same result could be achieved if the exposure were made with 1/100 sec. at *f*/18, or 1/50 sec. at *f*/25, or 1/1000 sec. at *f*/5.6, or with any number of different combinations of *f*/stop and shutter speed. In any given case, all the possible combinations of *f*/stop

Diaphragm and shutter

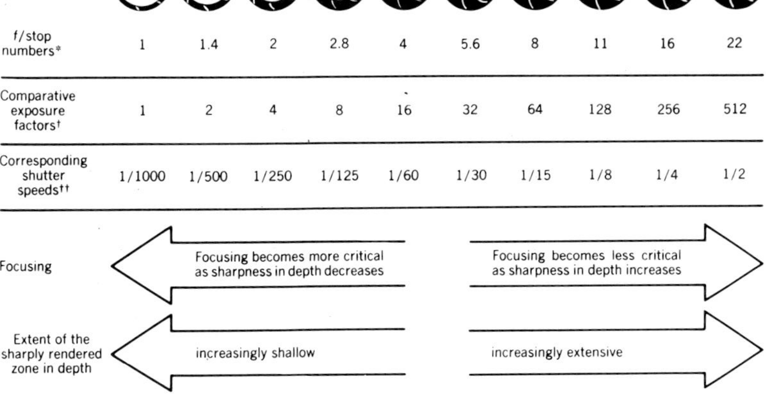

f/stop numbers*	1	1.4	2	2.8	4	5.6	8	11	16	22
Comparative exposure factors†	1	2	4	8	16	32	64	128	256	512
Corresponding shutter speeds††	1/1000	1/500	1/250	1/125	1/60	1/30	1/15	1/8	1/4	1/2

	←	→
Focusing	Focusing becomes more critical as sharpness in depth decreases	Focusing becomes less critical as sharpness in depth increases
Extent of the sharply rendered zone in depth	increasingly shallow	increasingly extensive
Rendition of a subject in motion	increasingly sharp	increasingly blurred
Conclusions	Hand-held exposures possible. The faster the subject motion, the higher the shutter speed necessary to prevent blur. Groundglass image brightens.	Use of a tripod required. The greater the subject depth, the higher the f/stop number required for adequate sharpness. Groundglass image darkens.

*Although an *f*/0.95 lens is available for 35mm cameras, at present no *f*/1 lens exists; this hypothetical lens is listed here only to complete the sequence.

†This sequence shows the relationship between *light transmission* by the lens (in accordance with the *f*/stop number sequence above) and *exposure time* (in accordance with the sequence of shutter speeds in fractions of a second below). For example: stopping down an *f*/1.4 lens to *f*/2.8 reduces its light transmission by a factor of 4—represented in this sequence by the ratio 2:8 = 1:4—with the result that if 1/500 sec. were the proper shutter speed at *f*/1.4, the correct shutter speed at *f*/2.8 would now be 4/500 = 1/125 sec. as indicated in the sequence below.

††The shutter-speed sequence listed here as an example would apply in actuality only if the combination of film speed and brightness of illumination required an exposure in accordance with EV (Exposure Value) 10. Under other conditions, of course, other shutter speeds would apply, a fact which, however, does not affect the following principle: stopping down the diaphragm from one *f*/number to the next higher one necessitates doubling the exposure time if the result of the exposure, in terms of image density and color rendition, is to remain the same.

For practical reasons, the listed shutter speeds don't always progress exactly by a factor of 2. For example, whereas 2/500 sec. is (correctly) listed as 1/250 sec. and 2/250 sec. as 1/125 sec., 2/125 sec. is listed as 1/60 sec. (instead of 1/62½ sec.) and 2/15 sec. as 1/8 sec. (instead of 1/7½ sec.). Such small inaccuracies have, of course, not the slightest influence on the exposure. As a matter of fact, shutter speed calibration is not uniform and varies with different makes of camera. For most practical purposes, 1/125 sec. and 1/100 sec. can be regarded as equal, as well as 1/60 and 1/50 sec., and 1/8 and 1/10 sec., particularly in view of the fact that due to manufacturing tolerances and mechanical wear, listed shutter speeds rarely correspond precisely to actual shutter speeds.

and shutter speed can be read off simultaneously on the dial of a correctly adjusted exposure meter, as will be explained on p. 70.

Covering power is that quality of a lens that determines the largest film size in conjunction with which it can be used. The greater its covering power, the larger the film size *in comparison with its focal length* which a specific lens will cover sharply. For example, wide-angle lenses cover negatives the diagonals of which are *longer* than their focal lengths, *i.e.*, they have great covering power. Telephoto lenses cover only negatives the diagonals of which are *shorter* than their focal lengths; thus they have relatively limited covering power. And most standard lenses have only sufficient covering power to cover satisfactorily the negative size for which they are designed. Therefore, when selecting a second or third lens for use in conjunction with a camera featuring interchangeability of lenses, a photographer must make sure that his new lens is capable of covering his negative size in its entirety.

Covering power is particularly important if a lens is to be used in conjunction with a view camera equipped with "swings," the use of which often necessitates throwing the lens axis off film center. In such a case, unless the lens has covering power to spare, part of the negative would be rendered unsharp or entirely blank (see illustrations on the opposite page). For this reason, experienced photographers, instead of working with a lens of standard focal length (say, six-inch with 4″ × 5″ film), use a six-inch wide-angle lens designed to cover the next larger film size (5″ × 7″). Since the focal lengths of both lenses are the same, image scale and perspective would also be the same in both cases; but the extra covering power of the six-inch wide-angle lens would guarantee pictures that are sharp all over even if "swings" are used in extreme positions.

The covering power of any lens increases with decreasing distance between subject and lens. As a result, in close-up photography, lenses with focal lengths too short to cover a given negative size when focused at infinity will cover it perfectly if the subject distance is sufficiently short. For example, a lens with a focal length of only one inch, originally designed to cover nothing larger than a 16mm movie camera frame, will sharply cover a 4″ × 5″ negative at a bellows extension (distance from lens center to film) of ten inches, rendering the subject (or the part of it shown) in nine times natural size.

Covering power

Lens in normal taking position

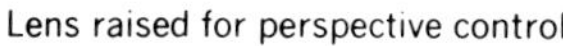

Lens raised for perspective control

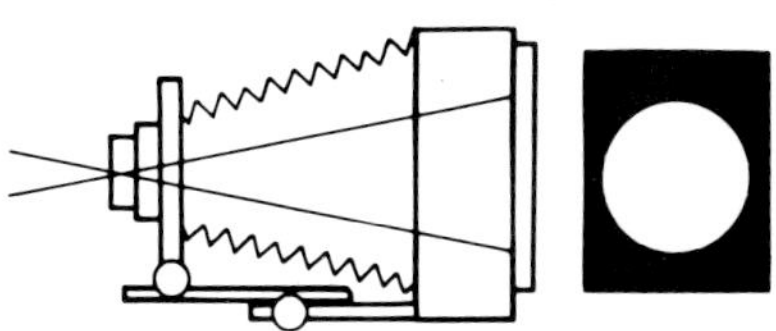

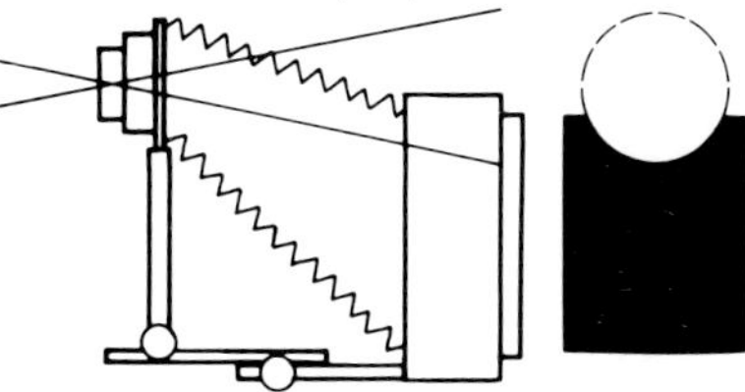

6-inch telephoto lens: covering power inadequate to cover fully the standard film size of 4″ × 5″.

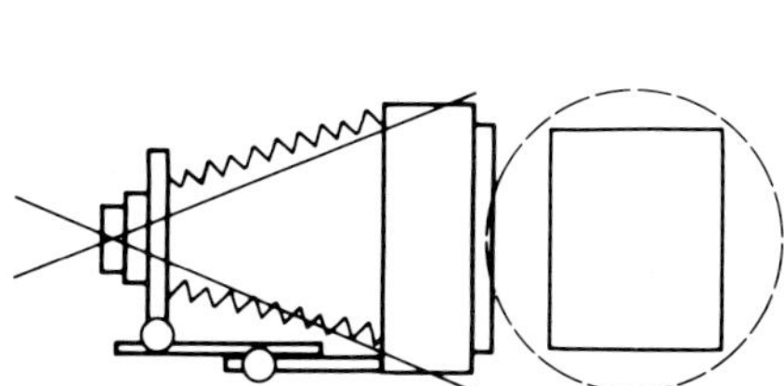

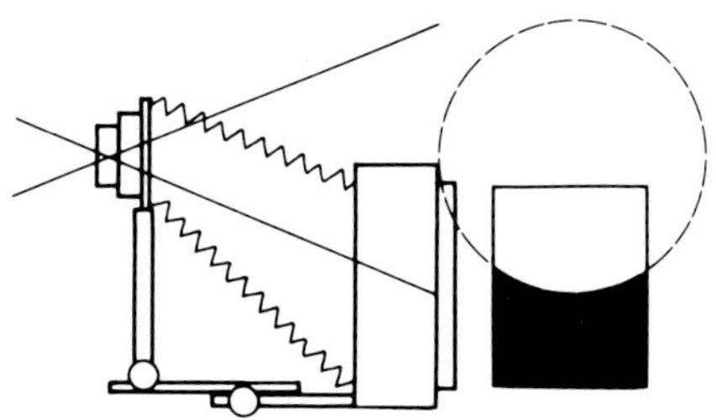

6-inch standard lens: covering power barely adequate to cover 4″ × 5″ in normal taking position, insufficient if lens is raised for perspective control.

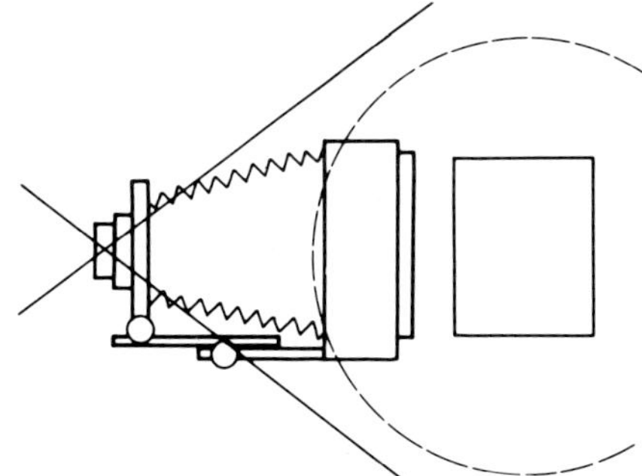

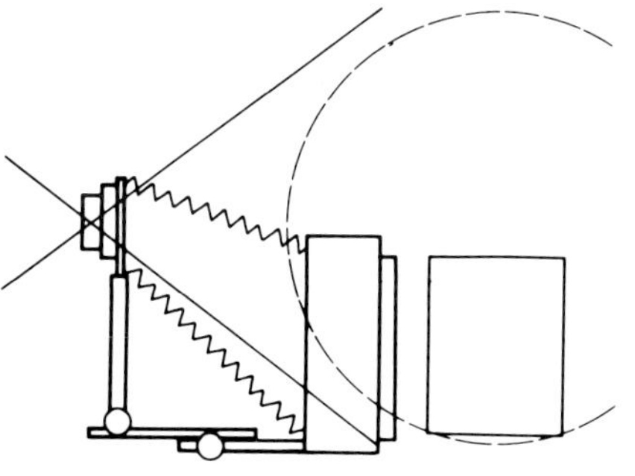

6-inch wide-angle lens: covering power adequate even if lens is fully raised for extreme perspective control.

The photograph of a piece of graph-paper at the right was taken with a 50mm lens on 4″ x 5″ film. It shows that every lens produces a circular image, only the center of which is sharp and therefore usable for photographic purposes. Consequently, the diameter of the sharply covered circle must be at least as long as the diagonal of the film format with which the respective lens is going to be used. If the covering power of a lens is insufficient for the intended purpose, the corners and edges of the picture will be either more or less unsharp, or entirely black, as indicated in the drawings above.

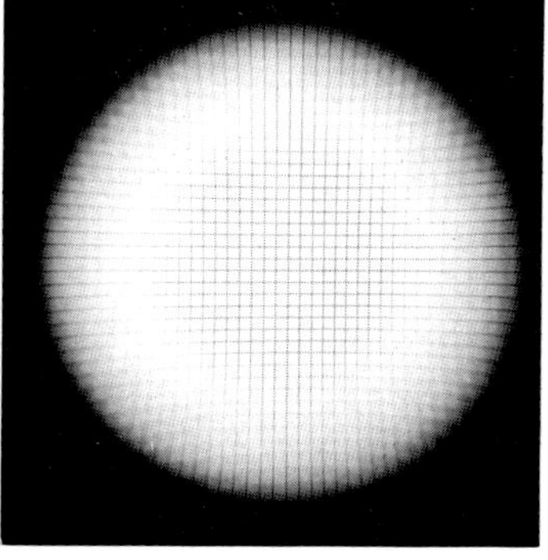

Lens PERFORMANCE

Provided a lens is suited to its task, its performance depends on the degree to which its designer was able to correct the seven basic faults or aberrations inherent in any lens design, and on the care with which it was manufactured and assembled. The most practical way for anyone without access to an optical laboratory to inform himself in this respect is to make a test. Take pictures of the kind for which you intend to use this lens, enlarge the negatives or project the slides, and analyze them in regard to the following qualities:

The degree of sharpness (pp. 34–36)
The degree of color correction (p. 36)
The degree of flare and fog (p. 38)
The evenness of light distribution (p. 38)
The degree of distortion (p. 38)

Please note that I specifically say "The degree of . . .," for a perfect lens does not exist. Furthermore, different photographers have different demands, and a lens that satisfies one may be rejected as inadequate by another. For example, a lens intended for copying must be sharper than a lens intended mainly for portraiture and photographing people, a type of work for which a slightly inferior lens will do just as well. A lens used for close-ups must be sharpest at relatively short subject distances, whereas a lens used in aerial or landscape photography must perform best when focused at infinity. A lens intended for architectural photography where straight lines prevail must be free of distortion, a fault that would go completely unnoticed in any kind of work not involving straight lines. And so on. It is for reasons like these that the common practice of testing lenses by photographing lens test charts or brick walls is of little practical value and sometimes even misleading. A lens that, because of curvature of field (see illustrations on the opposite page, bottom), performed badly when tested by photographing a chart—a flat, two-dimensional, relatively near object--may perform splendidly when used to photograph distant, three-dimensional subjects like landscapes.

Sharpness. In regard to sharpness, the performance of almost any lens can be improved by stopping down its diaphragm from two (slow lenses) to five (high-speed lenses) *f*/stops beyond the maximum aperture. Further stopping down will, of course, increase the extent of the sharply covered zone in depth (pp. 62–63), but usually will not improve the sharpness of rendition as such and may actually impair it.

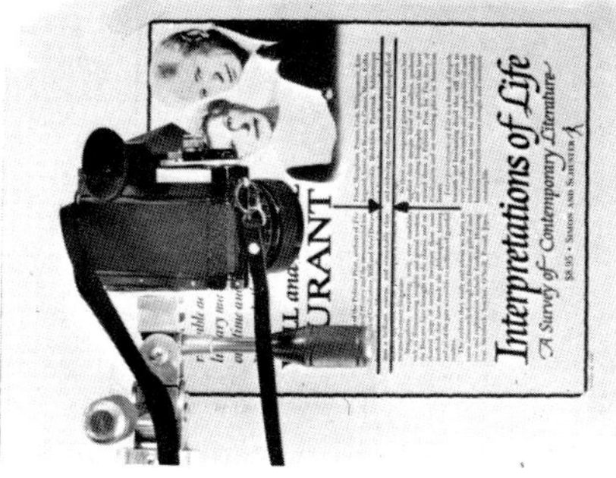

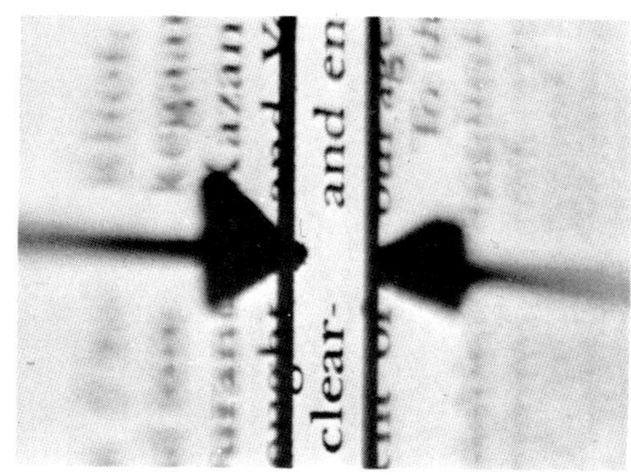

Even the sharpest lens is bound to produce unsharp pictures if the camera's focusing mechanism is out of adjustment. To check, mark a line of type on a well-printed magazine page by drawing black lines on either side of it, tape the page to the wall as shown in the photograph at the left, place the camera at an angle of approximately 45° to the test object, focus carefully on the target line, and take a picture with the diaphragm of the lens wide open.

If the marked line is sharpest, the focusing mechanism is "in sync" with the lens (photograph at the right). But if a line of type either in front of or behind the marked line appears sharper, the focusing mechanism is out of sync and must be adjusted before the camera can be expected to yield sharp pictures.

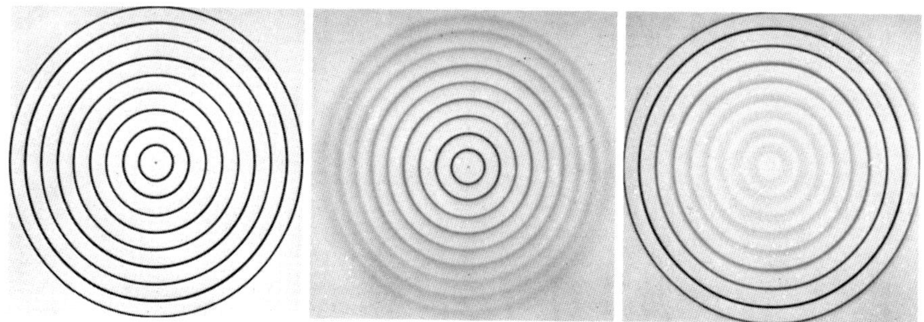

Curvature of field, the most common of all lens faults, can make it impossible to produce photographs in which the center and the edges of the picture are sharp simultaneously. The reason: the projected image of a flat object (like a test chart) does not lie in a flat plane but is curved like a saucer.

To test a lens for curvature of field, photograph a test chart consisting of concentric circles. If the lens is free of this fault, all circles will be rendered sharp simultaneously (picture at left). But if no more than two or three rings appear reasonably sharp (either the ones in the center, or those near the edges, depending on where you focused), while all the others appear more or less blurred, curvature of field is present. Stopping down the diaphragm reduces this effect somewhat but cannot eliminate it completely.

For clarity's sake, the center and righthand pictures were taken with a simple magnifier lens in which curvature of field is present to a very high degree; photographic lenses, even poor ones, show the effect to a much lesser degree.

As a rule, the sharpest lens type is the so-called "process apochromat" designed for copying and photomechanical reproduction work at relatively short subject distances; such lenses are also excellent for commercial product photography, particularly in color, but available only for 4″ × 5″ and larger cameras. Lenses specifically computed for use with small cameras are, as a rule, sharper than lenses intended for large cameras; the use of a lens designed for a 4″ × 5″ or larger camera in a small, focal-plane shutter equipped camera, although perfectly feasible, is normally not recommended. Most (but not all) high-speed lenses are less sharp than lenses of more moderate speed, even if the high-speed lens is stopped down to the same *f*/number as the lens of lower speed. In close-up photography, special close-up or true macro lenses yield somewhat sharper pictures than most regular lenses. A filter of inferior quality, fingerprints on the lens or filter, sloppy focusing, a rangefinder or mirror that is out of alignment, a shutter speed insufficiently high to "stop" subject motion, accidental camera movement during the exposure, or poor enlarging practices can make the sharpest lens yield unsharp pictures.

Color correction. Inadequate color correction manifests itself in the form of color fringes surrounding the outlines of objects and, in black-and-white photography, slightly fuzzy pictures. With the exception of lenses found only in cheap roll-film cameras, all modern lenses are sufficiently color corrected to satisfy average demands. Yet there are differences: *achromatic lenses* (the type to which most photographic lenses belong) are corrected to bring two colors of the spectrum into focus simultaneously; *apochromatic lenses* (intended primarily for high-class commercial color photography with large cameras and for photomechanical reproduction work) are corrected to bring three colors into focus simultaneously and produce somewhat superior results.

Professionals know that, although most lenses produce transparencies that are "neutral" in color, a few yield slides that are slightly yellowish ("warm") in tone, whereas others produce transparencies with a slightly bluish ("cold") overall tone. Such differences in overall color are due to differences in the composition of the optical glass or in the anti-reflex coating of the respective lenses and, if objectionable, can easily be corrected through permanent use of an appropriate filter.

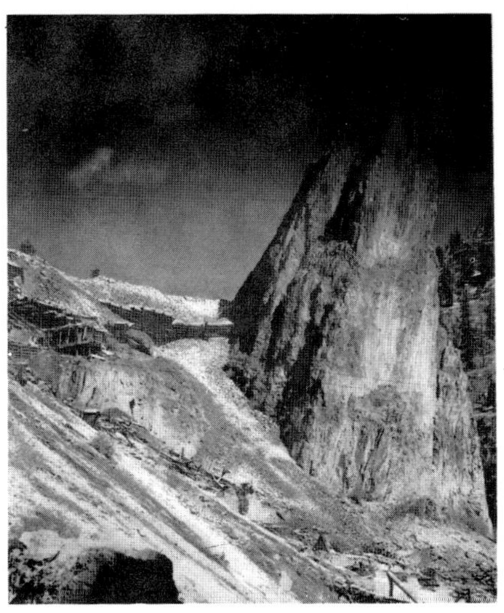

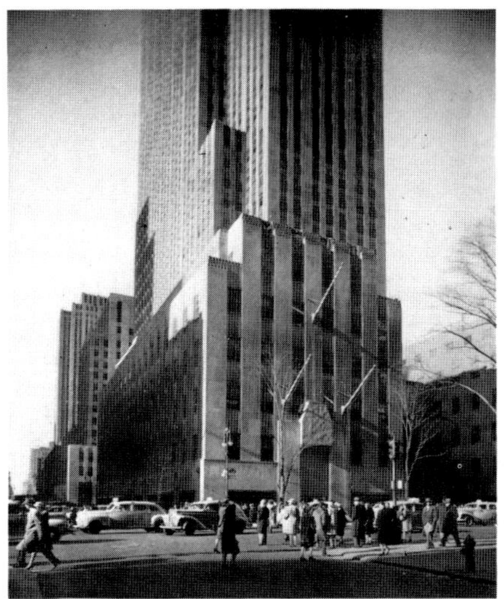

Insufficient covering power of the lens (see p. 32) caused the vignetting (cutting off of part of the picture) in the photo at the left and the unsharpness near the top of the building in the one at the right. In both cases, the lens of a view camera was raised in an effort to avoid "perspective distortion" and prevent "converging verticals," but inadequate covering power caused part of the picture to fall outside the usable field (see illustrations on p. 33). The result: two ruined photographs.

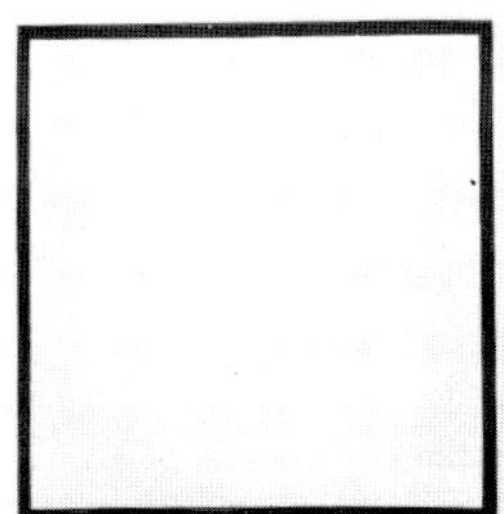

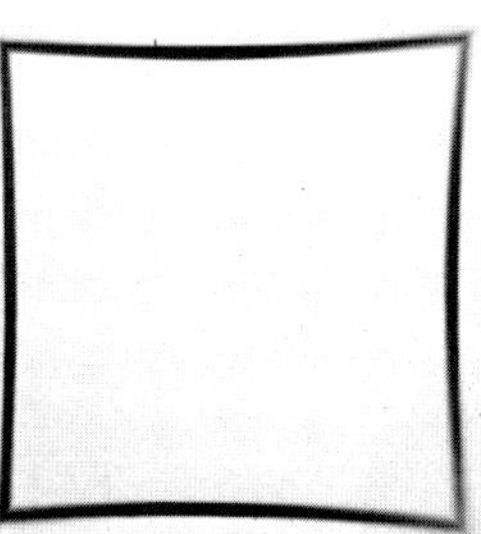

Curvilinear distortion is a fault particularly of wide-angle and zoom lenses. To test for it, photograph a square like the one at the left. Lenses free from curvilinear distortion will reproduce a square as a square, while those suffering from this fault will render its sides either curving inward (pincushion distortion) or outward (barrel distortion), as shown in the photographs in the center and at the right, respectively. Whereas this fault makes the lens so affected unsuitable for architectural and commercial photography, in which straight lines must be rendered straight, its effects are not noticeable in subjects that do not contain straight lines.

Flare and fog. Unavoidably, a certain amount of the light entering any lens is reflected by the surfaces of its elements, the inside of the lens mount, and internal parts of the camera, bounced back and forth and scattered before it reaches the film, not in the form of an image but as flare and fog. Flare manifests itself in the form of light spots that can have almost any shape and size but are usually crescentic, circular, fan-shaped, or repeating the form of the diaphragm aperture. Fog takes the form of a veil of haze that desaturates color and lowers the overall contrast of the negative or transparency. Although the practice of coating lenses with an anti-reflection compound has considerably minimized the danger of flare and fog, it has not eliminated it completely, and different lenses display this defect to different degrees. It is most common in lenses with a greater-than-average number of glass-to-air surfaces, zoom lenses, high-speed lenses, and lenses with unusually strong curvatures, and it is most likely to occur in backlighted photographs and those in which strong sources of light form part of the picture. Its presence, degree, or absence can only be revealed by tests.

Evenness of light distribution. All lenses deliver more light to the center of the film than to its edges and corners (which appear correspondingly darker in the picture), but the degree of this light falloff varies widely. Although virtually unnoticeable in most standard lenses, it can become quite pronounced, particularly in wide-angle lenses, especially in conjunction with color film which, because of its more limited contrast range, reacts more strongly to uneven light distribution than black-and-white film. This fault is most noticeable in pictures that contain large areas of uniform, medium-light color (or gray); its extent can only be revealed by tests.

Distortion. True distortion (which must not be confused with perspective distortion, which is the fault of the photographer) manifests itself by rendering actually straight lines as curves, an effect that becomes increasingly pronounced the farther the straight lines are from the center of the picture (where straight lines are rendered straight). This fault, most often found in the more extreme wide-angle lenses and in zoom lenses, can make a lens unsuitable for architectural and interior photography. However, in the absence of straight lines, this phenomenon, which is illustrated on p. 37, bottom, is not noticeable.

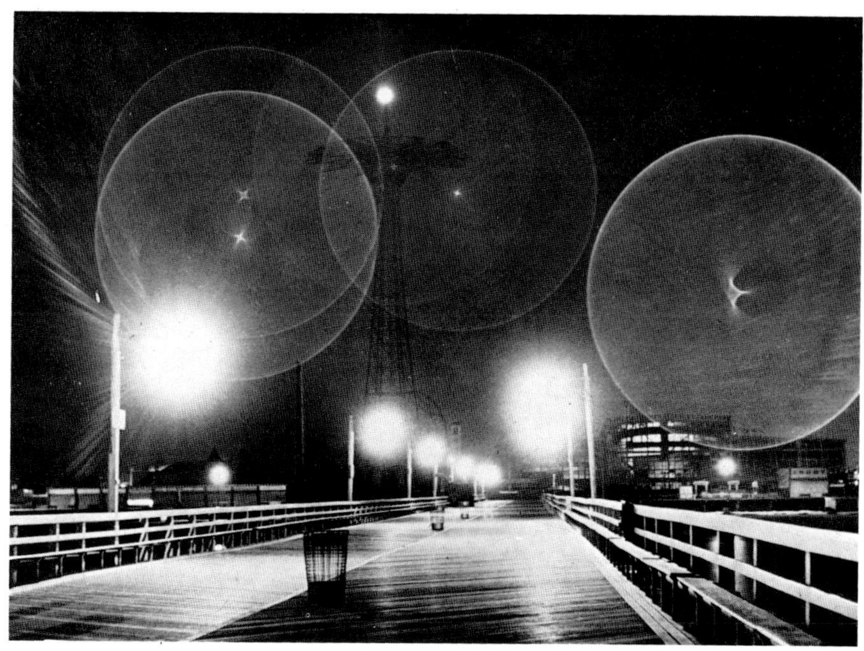

Typical manifestations of flare (p. 38) caused by direct light striking the lens. To avoid, when shooting toward a source of light that does not appear in the picture (otherwise, nothing can be done), use an effective lens shade or, with the aid of your hand or another suitable object, cast a shadow over the lens without, however, cutting off part of the picture.

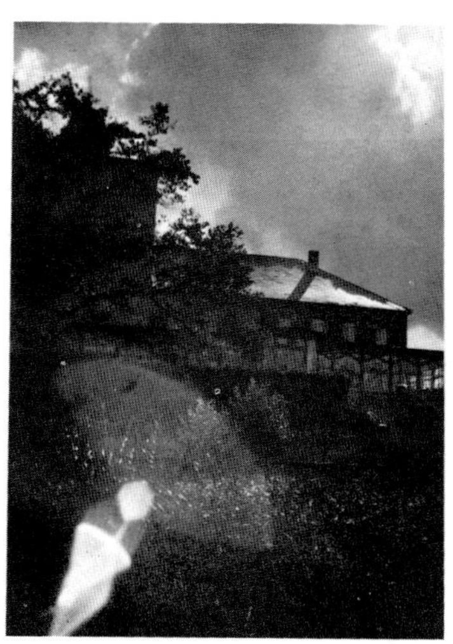

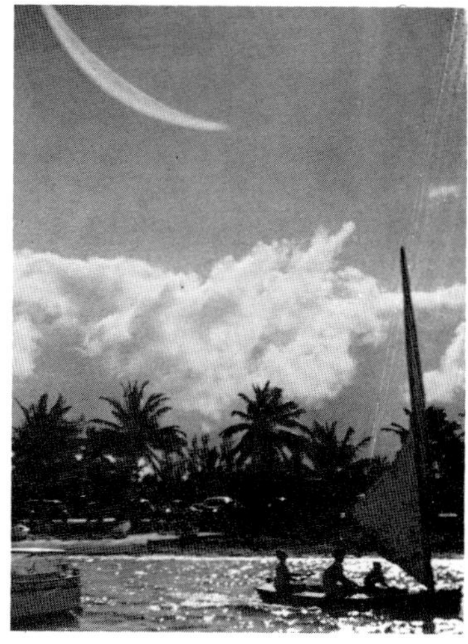

Lens TYPE

Photographers who choose their lenses on the basis of brand name and price alone invite potential disaster, for the most important quality of any lens is *suitability*. Neither "speed" nor cost nor fame means a thing if the lens is of a type unsuited to the type of work it has to perform. The following survey briefly discusses 13 different types of photographic lenses:

Lens type	Focal length
Standard lenses **High-speed lenses**	**standard focal length**
Wide-angle lenses **Close-up lenses**	**short focal length**
Process lenses **Soft-focus lenses**	**medium focal length**
Telephoto lenses **Monoculars** **Catadioptric lenses** **Aerial lenses**	**long focal length**
Zoom lenses **Slip-on lenses** **Teleconverters**	**variable focal length**

Standard lenses, characterized by speeds ranging from *f*/2 (35mm cameras) to *f*/5.6 (4″ × 5″ cameras) and focal lengths more or less equal to the diagonal of the film size they have to cover, produce pictures that in regard to angle of view and perspective conform most closely to the impressions we receive through our eyes. They are generally the most useful type of lens and should be the first lens a photographer who buys a camera featuring lens interchangeability should acquire.

High-speed lenses, characterized by speeds ranging from *f*/0.95 to *f*/1.8, are especially "bred" for "speed," often at the expense of other desirable lens qualities. As a result, in comparison with lenses of more normal speeds, high-speed lenses are always bigger, heavier, more expensive, and frequently less sharp and more prone to uneven light distribution, flare, and fog. They are indispensable in cases in which a large relative aperture (high lens speed) is of primary importance—photography under marginal light conditions, deliberate limitation of the sharply rendered zone in depth (pp. 62–63), "stopping" of fast subject motion through use of very high shutter speeds—but are not recommended for general photography.

Wide-angle lenses are characterized by shorter-than-normal focal lengths in conjunction with greater-than-normal covering power. Whereas standard lenses encompass angles of view of approximately 45°, wide-angle lenses cover angles that range from 60° to 180°. Similar to high-speed lenses, they are "bred" with one prime objective in mind—covering power—sometimes to the detriment of other desirable lens qualities. As a result, many wide-angle lenses are subject to uneven light distribution (p. 38) and distortion (pp. 38, 39), and those intended for use with 4″ × 5″ and larger cameras are relatively "slow." Wide-angle lenses come in two types:

Lenses computed to produce pictures in which perspective is rectilinear, *i.e.*, actually straight lines are rendered straight (except, of course, for the effects of distortion, if present in the respective lens). This type of wide-angle lens encompasses angles of view that range from 60° to 100° for lenses designed for use with cameras up to 4″ × 5″ and up to 130°—the Goerz Hypergon lenses—for 5″ × 7″ and 8″ × 10″ cameras.

Lenses computed to produce pictures in which perspective is spherical, *i.e.*, actually straight lines are rendered curved, increasingly so the farther they are from the center of the picture. These are the so-called "fish-eye," or "fish-eye type," lenses, most of which yield circular pictures encompassing angles of view that, depending on the respective lens, range from 150° to 180°, or more.

Wide-angle lenses are invaluable in cases in which circumstances make it impossible to encompass the desired large angle with a standard lens or when the typical wide-angle perspective ("exaggerated perspective" or "perspective distortion") is desired for emphasis. They are totally unsuited to general photography.

Close-up lenses are specially computed for maximum sharpness at subject distances that are measured in centimeters or inches rather than meters or feet. Also called "macro lenses" (although not every so-called "macro lens" is a "true" close-up lens), they sometimes feature lens mounts that permit focusing all the way down to rendition in natural size on the film without the aid of extension tubes or auxiliary bellows. Their focal lengths are usually short and their speeds relatively slow. Typical representatives are the Macro Kilars and the Zeiss Luminars.

Process lenses, characterized by relatively long focal lengths, low speeds, virtual absence of curvature of field (a common lens fault, see p. 35), and high prices, are designed to deliver the utmost in sharpness of rendition at fairly short subject distances. They are available only for 4″ × 5″ and larger cameras and are unsurpassed for reproduction of flat objects like documents or paintings, for commercial product photography, and for moderate close-ups of static subjects in general.

Soft-focus lenses produce pictures in which rendition is neither sharp nor unsharp but somewhere in between. Subject detail seems to consist of a relatively sharp nucleus surrounded by a halo of unsharpness, an effect that becomes more pronounced with increasing subject contrast and can be quite effective in high-contrast, backlighted shots.

This is an "old-fashioned," highly specialized lens type of very limited usefulness, which, however, still ranks high with certain pictorialists and photographers of women. Indiscriminately used, it leads to disaster.

Telephoto lenses are long-focus lenses of special design insofar as, focused at any subject distance, they require less extension (distance between lens and film) than ordinary lenses of comparable focal lengths, a characteristic that, of course, has practical advantages. Used from the same camera position, in comparison with a standard lens, a telephoto lens renders the subject in larger scale, the gain in image size being directly proportional to the focal lengths of the lenses: a telephoto lens of twice the focal length of a given standard lens will render the subject twice as large on the film.

Telephoto lenses are used to produce pictures in sufficiently large scale in cases in which the distance between subject and camera is so great that a lens of shorter focal length would fail or when a photographer wishes to exploit the "monumental" effect of the typical telephoto perspective (in which case, he may have to increase deliberately the distance between the subject and himself in order to be able to use his telephoto lens). Moderate telephoto lenses also give excellent results in portrait photography. All telephoto lenses magnify not only the subject but also the effects of accidental camera movement during exposure, a fact that makes it imperative to hold a telephoto lens equipped camera extra steady (p. 61) when taking the picture.

Monoculars, binoculars, and prism scopes, used in conjunction with any 35mm or 2¼″ × 2¼″ single-lens reflex camera, enable a photographer to produce at relatively low cost pictures in greatly and even enormously enlarged scale. This can be done in one of two ways:

Monophotography—This technique is applicable only to cameras providing for lens interchangeability. After removing the original lens, the photographer takes the picture using only the monocular or scope. Advantages over the following method are simpler and more rigid setup, no need for delicate adjustments since the monocular or scope is connected directly to the camera body by means of an adapter tube, less danger of vignetting (cutting off the corners of the image), and higher optical quality.

Binophotography—The monocular or scope is used in front of the regular lens. This technique is applicable to SLR's with non-removable lenses and TLR's but, in comparison with monophotography, has the following drawbacks: clumsy adapter mounts requiring careful alignment must be used; inferior sharpness of the image, which usually is more or less circular due to extensive vignetting and shows considerable light falloff toward its perimeter.

Catadioptric lenses are combination lens-mirror systems based on the principle of the reflecting telescope. They are practicable only in focal lengths of 20 inches (500mm) or longer and have three main advantages over telephoto lenses of comparable focal lengths: they are much more compact, much lighter, and almost completely color corrected. Their main disadvantage is the fact that their design precludes the use of a diaphragm, *i.e.*, they cannot be "stopped down." As a result, the sharply covered zone in depth is always extremely shallow, and the exposure must be regulated either by adjusting the shutter speed accordingly or with the aid of special neutral-density filters provided by the lens manufacturer.

Aerial lenses are so highly specialized in design that they are virtually useless for anything except aerial photography. Many are too heavy to be practical in conjunction with ordinary "terrestrial" cameras and too large to fit into conventional leaf-type shutters. Furthermore, all aerial lenses are computed to yield maximum sharpness when focused at infinity and usually perform badly at near distances; many are designed for use in conjunction with a deep red filter, without which they are not very sharp due to residual chromatic aberration, a drawback that makes them unfit for color photography.

Zoom lenses, which can be used only in conjunction with 35mm SLR's, are complex optical systems with variable focal lengths. Depending on the design, the longest focal length is two, three, or even four times as long as the shortest, with an infinite number of intermediary focal lengths available in between. As a result, zoom lenses provide within one unit the equivalent of many lenses, thereby saving the photographer weight, space, money, and the time otherwise required to change from one lens to another. In addition, they enable him to study his subject from one camera position in many different scales and forms of cropping simply by sliding a collar or turning a ring. Disadvantages are bulkiness and weight, plus the fact that most zoom lenses are less sharp than comparable telephoto lenses and are often subject to distortion.

Slip-on lenses, which are designed to fit in front of standard lenses, are auxiliary lenses, the purpose of which is to alter the characteristics of the lenses in conjunction with which they are used. They are available in different types to increase and decrease, respectively, the focal length of the primary lens, to convert it into a fish-eye lens (p. 41), or to make it act like a soft-focus lens (p. 42). Their purpose is to widen the scope of photographers restricted to working with cameras with fixed lenses by enabling them to produce, within certain limits, the effects normally achieved only with the aid of interchangeable lenses of more or less special design.

Teleconverters (or focal-length extenders) are auxiliary lenses which, inserted between the camera body and a standard or telephoto lens, increase the focal length of the primary lens by a factor that ranges from 1.85 to 3, depending on the converter's design. Their use is, at least at present, restricted to 35mm SLR's with interchangeable lenses. Although adequate for many purposes, the sharpness of the so-produced pictures is usually somewhat inferior to that of pictures made with telephoto lenses of comparable focal lengths.

HOW TO CHOOSE YOUR EXPOSURE METER

Correct exposure is an indispensable requirement for the production of satisfactory color photographs. Three aids are available to help a photographer achieve this goal:

Exposure tables, which are included with every package of film, interpret light conditions in terms of everyday experience. Within the limit of their applicability, they provide adequate instructions for photographing ordinary subjects under ordinary conditions. For certain kinds of subjects (for example, photographs of fireworks and at night), exposure tables are the *only* guides to correct exposure.

Exposure meters built into the camera provide the simplest and fastest way of achieving correct exposure. In comparison with exposure tables, they have a wider range of applicability and are more precise. In comparison with separate, hand-held exposure meters, they are more convenient. Furthermore, since they measure the intensity of the light *after* it has passed through the lens, they automatically compensate for possible light losses caused by filters or additional extension between lens and film in close-up photography—factors that the user of a hand-held exposure meter must include in his calculations but cannot measure directly. On the other hand, if belonging to the integrating type (p. 46), they are less convenient for establishing the contrast range of the subject.

Separate, hand-held exposure meters, although generally less convenient to use than built-in meters, are potentially more accurate (except in regard to close-up photography), enable a photographer to measure the contrast range (p. 75) of his subject (exception: incident-light meters, see p. 46), and, since they are available in many different types, offer a wider choice of different methods of measurement. Whereas built-in exposure meters are generally powered by cadmium-sulfide (CdS) cells (p. 46) in conjunction with batteries and designed to measure *only* reflected light, hand-held meters, in addition to CdS types, are also available in the form of meters powered by selenium cells and meters designed to measure the incident light (p. 46).

Exposure meters come in the following types and designs, each with its own advantages and drawbacks:

Reflected-light meters measure the brightness of the light reflected by the subject. They are available in the form of integrating meters, spot meters, hand-held meters, and built-in meters powered either by selenium or cadmium-sulfide cells. To provide a reading, they must be *pointed at the subject from the camera position.* In contrast to incident-light meters, they enable a photographer to establish the contrast range of his subject by taking separate readings of its lightest and darkest parts.

Incident-light meters measure the brightness of the light that illuminates the subject. They are integrating meters available only in the form of hand-held meters powered either by a selenium or a cadmium-sulfide cell. To provide a reading, they must be *pointed at the camera from the subject position.* They are somewhat easier to use than reflected-light meters but do not permit a photographer to establish the contrast range of his subject.

Integrating meters integrate the reflectance of all the parts of the subject from the lightest to the darkest or all the light sources that contribute to the illumination into a single averaged reading, a characteristic that makes them easy to use but complicates (reflected-light meters) or prohibits (incident-light meters) their use as instruments for establishing the contrast range of the subject.

Spot meters, which have a very narrow angle of acceptance, are reflected-light meters that selectively measure only a very small area of the subject. This makes them particularly well suited to establishing the contrast range of the subject but difficult to use correctly for inexperienced photographers, who might base their exposure on unsuitable measurements.

Selenium cell powered meters require no batteries (which may go "dead"), last virtually forever, and are somewhat easier to use than CdS meters but are also larger, more delicate, and less sensitive at very low light levels.

Cadmium-sulfide cell (CdS) powered meters require a battery (which normally lasts a year or longer), are smaller, more rugged, and more sensitive than selenium cell meters but are subject to "fatigue" and "needle-creep."

HOW TO CHOOSE YOUR COLOR FILTERS

The purpose of a color filter is to change the response of a photographic emulsion to color and light. This may become necessary for one of two reasons:

1. Natural-appearing color rendition can be expected only if film and light are compatible, but the three available types of color film are "balanced" only for use with four specific types of light: standard daylight (p. 92), electronic flash (p. 52), photoflood lamps (3400 K, see p. 50), and professional tungsten lamps (3200 K, see p. 50). However, dozens of other types of light exist, ranging from non-standard daylight (pp. 92–93) and ordinary household illumination to fluorescent light. To achieve natural-appearing color rendition, the light emitted by such non-conforming sources must be "corrected" to conform to the standard of the respective film. The means for this are color filters.

2. Creative photographers are often not satisfied with color rendition under standardized conditions; they demand more interesting, significant, or unusual effects. Perhaps they wish to give their pictures a "warmer" and more yellowish or a "cooler" and more bluish tone, or present their subject in a lavender light, in order to create a specific mood. In such cases, they can realize their intentions with the aid of the appropriate color filter.

The effect of a color filter upon a photographic emulsion is twofold: it changes the response of the film to color and light as explained above, and it may prolong the exposure. The reason for the latter is that, in order to be effective, a filter has to absorb certain wavelengths of the incident light. The result, of course, is that less light is now available for the exposure than if no filter had been used, the amount lost depending upon the color sensitivity of the film, the color (spectral composition) of the light, and the color and density of the filter. To provide a basis for accurate exposure calculation, film manufacturers have assigned specific factors to specific film-filter-light combinations by which the exposure must be multiplied if underexposure is to be avoided. These factors are listed in the instructions packed with each filter.

Kodak Color Conversion filters enable a photographer to use a color film in conjunction with a type of light for which it is *not* intended. Provided the exposure is multiplied by the respective factor, the following film-filter-light combinations produce satisfactory results:

daylight color film + 80A + 3200 K tungsten lamps
daylight color film + 80B + 3400 K photoflood lamps
daylight color film + 80C + clear-glass flashbulbs
Type A color film + 85 + standard daylight
Type B color film + 85B + standard daylight

Kodak Light Balancing filters enable a photographer to change "off-color" light into the type of light for which his color film is balanced. Daylight, for example, is yellowish early in the morning and late in the afternoon; bluish on overcast days. To make it conform to "white" or "standard" daylight (p. 24), two sets of light-balancing filters are available: Kodak Filters 81, which are reddish, come in eight different densities, and must be used if the daylight contains too much blue; Kodak Filters 82, which are blue, come in four different densities, and must be used if the daylight contains too much yellow or red. More about the use of these filters on p. 87.

Kodak Color Compensating filters enable a photographer to more or less "correct" oddball light sources like fluorescent light; to compensate for deviations from normal color balance of a particular film emulsion; to correct unsatisfactory color rendition in cases in which exposures are abnormally long or short (reciprocity failure); to balance the light source of his enlarger when making color prints; and to change, influence, and control the overall color balance of his transparencies and prints. Designed as Series CC filters, Kodak Color Compensating filters come in different densities in the colors yellow, magenta, cyan, red, green, and blue.

Ultraviolet filters (haze or skylight filters) absorb ultraviolet radiation, which, though invisible to the eye, would cause color photographs of distant scenery to appear too blue.

Polarizers mitigate or eliminate glare and reflections on shiny nonmetallic surfaces like glass, water, polished wood, etc., and provide the only means by which a pale blue sky can be rendered somewhat darker in a color photograph. Examples of the use of polarizers are given on pp. 90–91.

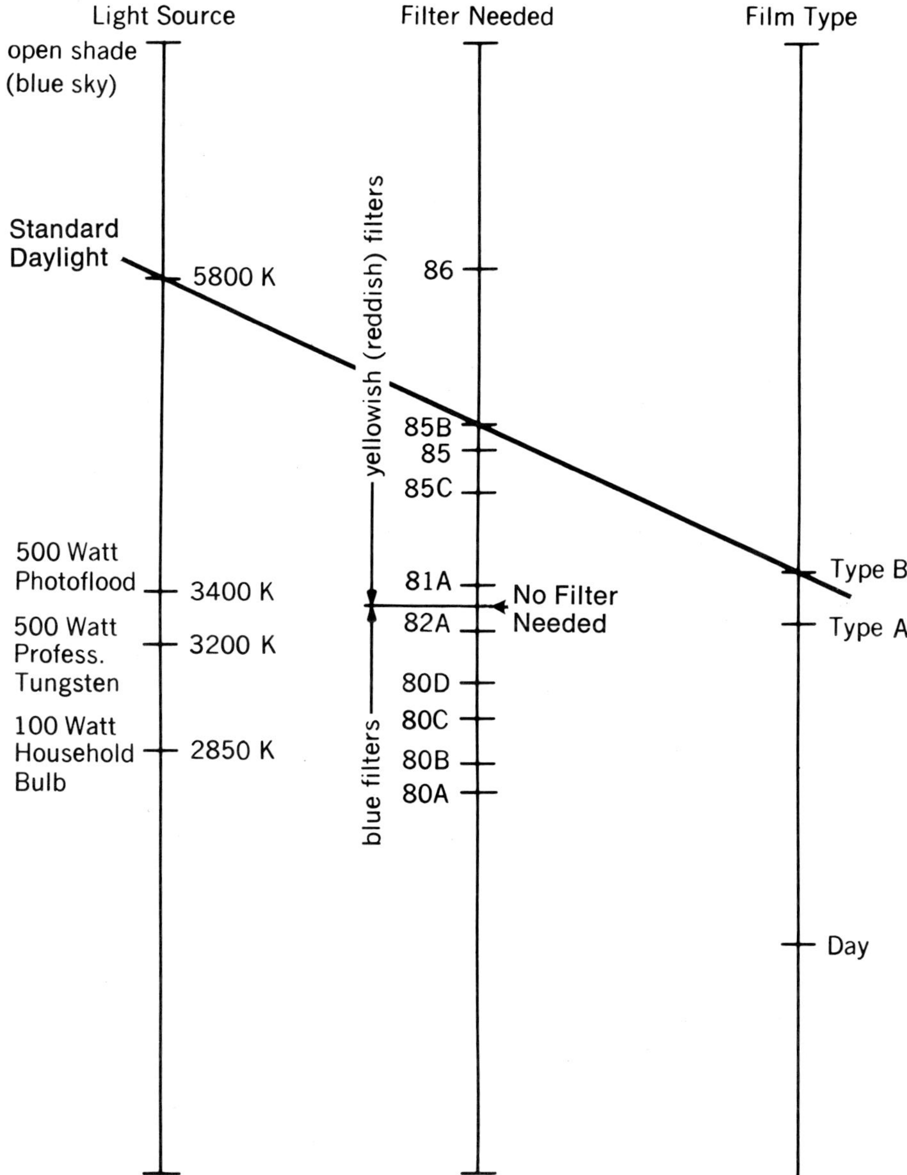

Perhaps the simplest way to determine the correct light-balancing filter is by means of the color filter Nomograph printed above. Place a straightedge across the Nomograph, connecting the type of color film to be used with the type of light in which the picture will be made. The required filter can then be found at the point where this line intersects the central column. For example, the combination of Type B color film and daylight requires an 85B filter. (See also p. 87.)

HOW TO CHOOSE YOUR LIGHTING EQUIPMENT

Lighting equipment for photographic purposes ranges all the way from flashcubes and strobes (electronic flash) small enough to be mounted on a 35mm camera to lamps and electronic flash assemblies sufficiently powerful to light up entire convention halls. Which type of lighting equipment a photographer needs depends, of course, on the kind of work he intends to do. In this respect, all a beginner may require is a small flash outfit to "fill in" shadows in daylight shots, particularly when taking close-ups of people (pp. 98–99). Someone intending to photograph interiors would need a number of photoflood lamps; a portraitist a combination of flood lamps and spotlights (pp. 100–101); and so on. The following survey of photo lamps should guide the reader in his choice.

Lamps producing continuous light

These lamps have the following advantages over lamps producing discontinuous light: the photographer can see the effect and measure the brightness of his illumination; with the aid of a reflected-light exposure meter, he can check the contrast range of his subject and thereby avoid overlighted and underlighted areas; he can control visually the distribution of light and shadow; he can make sure that the background receives sufficient light. On the other hand, lamps producing continuous light are normally not bright enough to permit action-stopping shutter speeds and, except for fluorescent tubes, produce a lot of heat. Distinguish among the following types:

3400 K photoflood lamps and reflector floods are suitable for general illumination and shadow fill-in in conjunction with Type A color films. For explanation of the term "3400 K" see p. 86.

3200 K professional tungsten lamps and reflector floods are suitable for general illumination and shadow fill-in in conjunction with Type B color films.

4800 K blue photoflood lamps are designed as supplementary illumination and to lighten (fill in) shadows in interior shots where the main illumination is provided by daylight coming in through windows. They are intended for use with daylight color films.

3400 K and 3200 K tungsten-halogen lamps produce an intensely bright light suitable for general illumination in conjunction with Type A and Type B color films, respectively. They are powered either by a.c. house current or by a battery pack and can therefore be used indoors, outdoors for daylight shadow fill-in, and at night.

Spotlights concentrate the light of a projection-type filament lamp by means of a spherical mirror behind and a condenser or Fresnel lens in front of the bulb. They produce a more contrasty type of illumination with deeper and more sharply defined shadows than flood lamps. In combination with flood lamps, they are excellent as main lights and accent lights (p. 100), less suited to general illumination unless a rather harsh effect is desired, and useless as fill-in lights. They come in many sizes, are normally adjustable for throwing a wider or narrower beam of light, and, if equipped with 3200 K bulbs, are suitable for use with Type B color films.

Fluorescent tubes emit light that is deficient in red and therefore unsuited to color photography, producing transparencies usually characterized by a muddy, greenish cast. This cast can be mitigated, changed to a different color, but rarely eliminated with the aid of color filters. The type of filter or combination of filters required depends on the type of fluorescent tube and the type of color film; follow the respective film manufacturer's recommendations.

Lamps producing discontinuous light

These lamps have the great advantage that they enable a photographer to "stop" motion, no matter how fast. On the other hand, they have the serious drawback that he cannot see in advance precisely where the shadows will fall (although large electronic flash lamps feature small, built-in "modelling lights," which somewhat facilitate setting up the lamps correctly); that he cannot establish the contrast range of his subject with an exposure meter; and that he normally cannot measure the brightness of the illumination but must instead determine the exposure on the basis of guide numbers (p. 52). For professionals, large, rather expensive strobe light meters are available. Consequently, whereas lamps producing continuous light are best for illuminating static subjects, lamps producing discontinuous light are best for illuminating dynamic subjects (people and action). Distinguish between the following two types:

Electronic flash (speedlight). Designed for use with daylight color films in cameras equipped with "X"-synchronization and powered either by batteries or a.c. house current, these lamps are equipped with repeating-type flash-tubes lasting several thousand flashes before they have to be replaced. Flash duration, which, depending on the model, ranges from 1/500 to 1/5000 sec. and shorter, is short enough to "stop" any subject motion and prevent blur due to inadvertent camera movement during exposure. In comparison with flashbulbs, the main advantages of electronic flash are lower operational cost, higher motion-stopping power, and greater convenience. Drawbacks are higher initial cost, relatively low light output (particularly in smaller units), and restriction of synchronization with focal-plane shutters to relatively low speeds.

Flashbulbs are designed to give one burst of light, then burn out. Blue (lacquered) flashbulbs are suitable for use with daylight color films; clear flashbulbs require the use of a color filter (consult the Nomograph on p. 49). Focal-plane shutter equipped cameras require the use of special "FP"-type flashbulbs; cameras equipped with between-the-lens shutters can be used with all except "FP"-type flashbulbs. The size of a flashbulb determines its light output: the larger, the more light. Flashbulbs are normally fired by batteries and "synchronized" with the aid of a flashgun to insure that maximum light output coincides with maximum shutter opening. In comparison with electronic flash, flashbulbs have the advantages of lower initial cost of the outfit, much higher light output relative to size and weight, and suitability for synchronization at any shutter speed. Drawbacks are inferior motion-stopping power, space requirements of the bulbs, and the fact that bulbs have to be changed after each shot.

Exposure with flash, both electronic and bulb, is calculated with the aid of guide numbers assigned by the flash equipment manufacturers to their products and listed in the data that accompany them. In conjunction with a film of a specific ASA rating (and, in the case of flashbulbs, a predetermined shutter speed), the *f*/stop required for correct exposure is found with the aid of the following formula:

$$f/\text{stop} = \frac{\text{guide number}}{\text{distance in feet between subject and flash}}$$

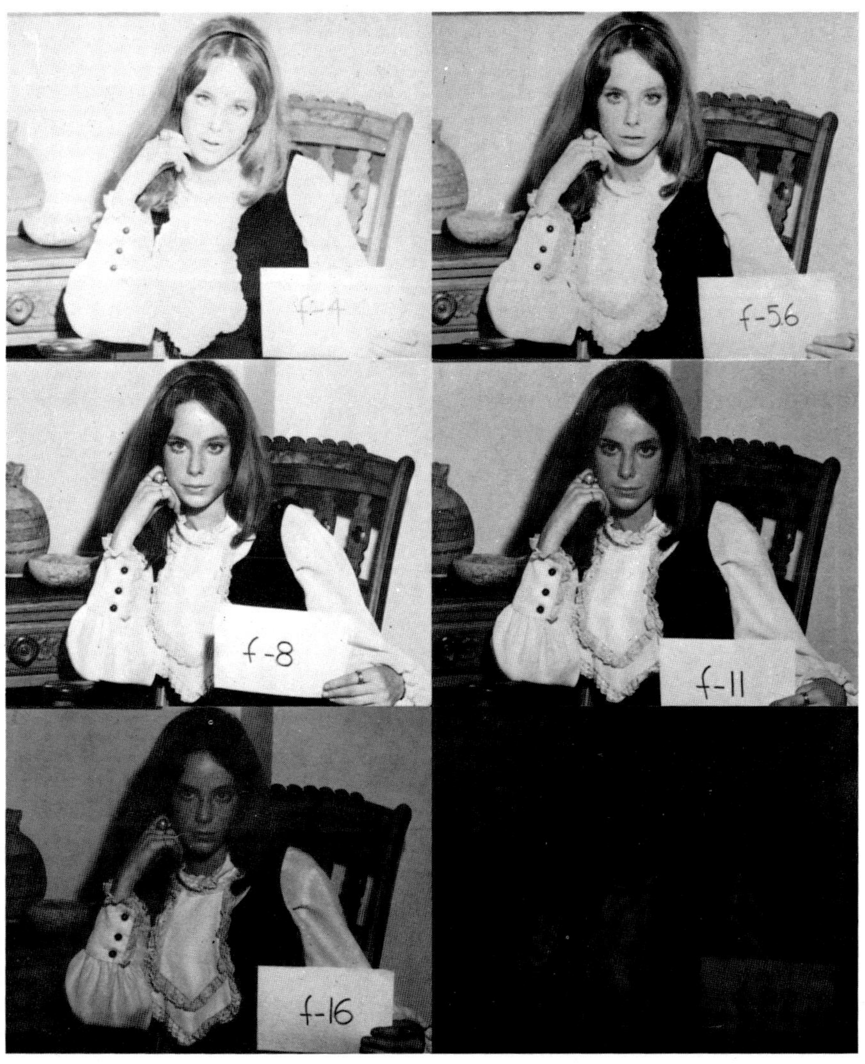

Whereas guide numbers for flashbulbs are usually reliable, those for speedlights are often overly optimistic and too high. To check, place a model X feet from the flash-equipped camera. Shoot a series of pictures with different *f*/stops under otherwise identical conditions. Multiply the *f*/stop number that produced the best picture by X; this is the "true" guide number for the combination of flash, film speed, and shutter speed used in the test.

Reflectors and diffusers. Used in a large reflector, the same lightbulb casts less sharply defined shadows than when mounted in a small reflector; it produces still softer light if used in a large reflector equipped with a diffuser, provided the diffuser is *larger* than the reflector and mounted four or five inches in front of it. Equipping a reflector with a diffuser of identical size mounted in contact with its rim does not diffuse the light appreciably but merely dims it. All of which goes to show that selection of the proper reflector and diffuser is as important as choosing the right kind of photo lamp.

Light stands. To be able to deploy his lamps efficiently, a photographer needs a light stand for each. He also should have at least one boom light, *i.e.*, an outrigger-like rod carrying a photo lamp at one end, mounted atop a light stand for overhead illumination. It is particularly useful in portraiture and small-object photography. Highly practical also are alligator clamps, which permit a photographer to clamp a photo lamp to furniture, a door, a ladder, etc., and swivel it into position. A number of extension cords and a "spider-box"—a multiple outlet into which to plug his wires—complete his lighting equipment.

EQUIPMENT TO WIDEN THE SCOPE OF YOUR WORK

Acquisition of a few additional pieces of equipment can often enable a photographer to widen the scope of his work completely out of proportion to the moderate extra cost involved. For example, spending a few dollars on a set of extension tubes opens to him the fascinating world of close-up photography; the purchase of a tripod enables him to explore the realm of time exposures or night photography; and so on. Therefore, I recommend that he consider the following items:

Extension tubes or **auxiliary bellows** extend the focusing range of 35mm and 2¼″ × 2¼″ SLR cameras that provide for interchangeability of lenses, making them suitable for photomacrography, *i.e.*, the taking of pictures in which a small object—an insect, a flower, a shell—is rendered in near-natural, natural, or greater-than-natural size on the film.

A reflex-housing transforms a 35mm rangefinder camera that provides for interchangeability of lenses into a single-lens reflex camera with most of its advantages (p. 12), making it suitable for close-up and extreme telephotography.

A tripod is an indispensable necessity for many types of photographic work: night photography; photography with a view camera (p. 14); any kind of photography involving serious perspective control (35mm SLR's equipped with a Nikkor PC or Schneider Curtagon lens permit a limited degree of perspective control); exposures involving shutter speeds longer than approximately 1/30 sec.; copy work and the making of reproductions of paintings, sculpture, and other works of art—all these require the use of a tripod.

Tripods come in a bewildering variety of different models, most of them shoddy, although not necessarily cheap. A wobby tripod, or one with locking nuts that tend to "freeze," is worse than useless—a liability. The best tripod is always the strongest, the one with the thickest legs; unfortunately, it is also the heaviest and most expensive. Two very useful features are a center post (called an "elevator"), which can be raised or lowered either by hand or with a crank, and a separate adjustment for levelling the camera laterally. For those who consider a tripod too big or heavy to carry around (although they use one indoors), I recommend one of the versatile tabletop tripods (which fit into a gadget bag), the best of which is made by Leitz; pressed hard against any rigid surface, no matter whether horizontal, vertical, or slanting, smooth or irregular, it provides sufficiently firm support for cameras up to 2¼″ × 2¼″ large. For action photography with a long telephoto lens, a gunstock-like camera support is sometimes very helpful.

Gadget bag. To carry his equipment conveniently and safely, a photographer needs a gadget bag. Personally, I like my bag too large rather than too small and prefer a flap lid to a zipper top. An inner tray, a separate top compartment, or one or two outside pockets to hold the exposure meter, film, and small accessories or other useful items, such as a notebook, pencil, or tape, eliminate the need for frequent "digging" in the main compartment of the bag. Unless a bag is "fitted," loose pieces of foam rubber are excellent for separating the various objects and protecting them from shock and abrasion.

II. The Technique of Color Photography

Even the finest photographic equipment is wasted if its owner does not know how to utilize its potential. This is so because the making of any good photograph involves three essential factors: suitable equipment, technical know-how in regard to its use, and artistic talent so that knowledge can be transformed into performance. The first of these three essentials was the subject of Part I, the second will be dealt with in the following section, and the third in Part III.

In regard to technical know-how, making a photograph involves the following steps:

AIMING THE CAMERA

As far as the average beginner is concerned, aiming a camera consists of centering the subject in the viewfinder, pushing the shutter release button, and considering the operation successful if he didn't cut off his victim's head.

In contrast to this happy-go-lucky approach, experienced photographers equate aiming with viewing and composing—a deliberate process of analytically evaluating the subject in its entirety, including its foreground and background, with the objective of not only "getting it on the film" but recording it in the most expressive form. They pay particular attention to such factors as perspective and possible distortion; juxtaposition and overlapping of individual picture elements; distribution of light and shadow, including the location of light sources that might cause flare or halation (p. 38); superfluous or distracting subject matter with special attention to disturbing objects in the background. They know that once the shutter has been released the die is cast, for better or for worse, and very little can be done afterwards to improve the picture.

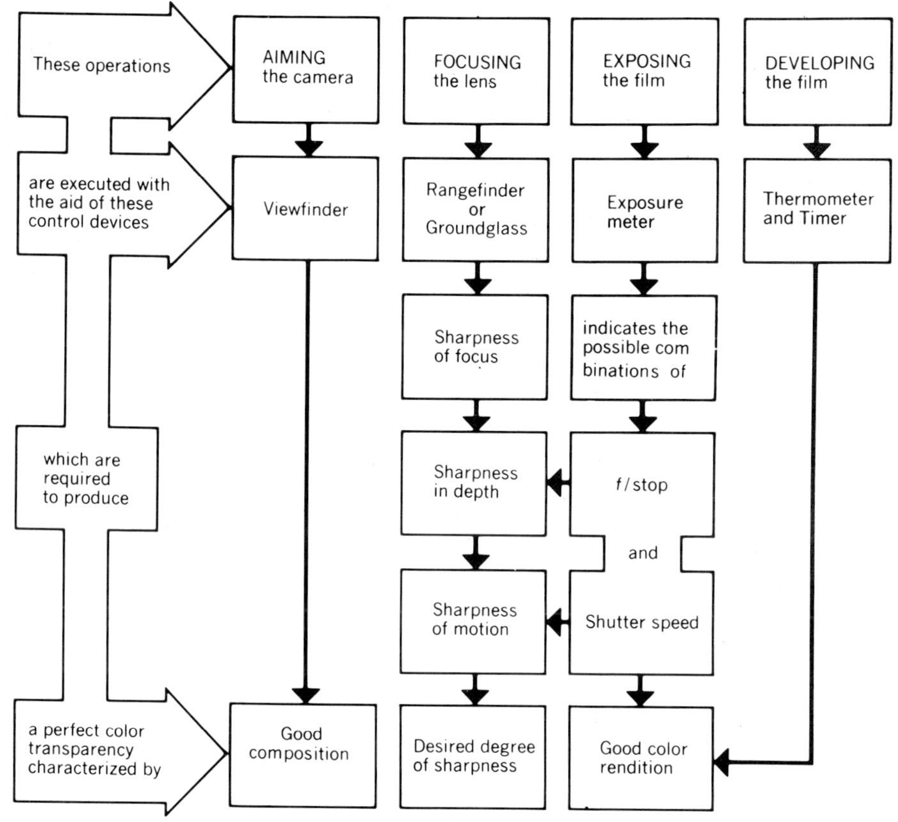

The diagram above indicates the interrelationship of the "technical" factors that decide the graphic appearance of a transparency. In this respect, *aiming* the camera with the aid of the viewfinder determines the composition; *focusing* the lens with the aid of the rangefinder or groundglass determines whether the subject will be rendered sharp or blurred; the *exposure*—the combined result of f/stop and shutter speed—in conjunction with correctly timed *development* with all the solutions at the proper temperature determines whether color in the transparency will be either "natural' and "good" or "unnatural" and "bad," *i.e.*, too light, too dark, or otherwise different from that of the subject. And finally, the *f*/stop, arrived at with the aid of the exposure meter (as part of the correct exposure), determines the extent of the sharply rendered zone in depth, whereas the *shutter speed*, also arrived at with the aid of the exposure meter (as part of the correct exposure), determines whether subject motion will be "stopped" or rendered in the form of a blur.

FOCUSING THE LENS

The purpose of focusing is to adjust the distance between lens and film in such a way that the image of the subject will be sharp (in focus): the shorter the distance between subject and lens, the longer the distance between lens and film, and vice versa. If the subject is very far away (at "infinity," which in practice means farther than approximately 300 feet), the distance between lens and film is for ordinary lenses equal to their focal length (p. 26)—the shortest distance at which a lens can still produce a sharp picture.

The means of focusing consist of two controls: *a mechanical device* (a helical focusing mount, a geared focusing knob, or a rack and pinion drive in conjunction with a bellows), which enables the photographer to adjust the distance between lens and film; and *an optical device* (a rangefinder or groundglass), which lets him see the precise moment at which the lens has been moved far enough to produce a sharp image of the subject on which it is focused. For specific information, consult the instruction booklet that accompanies your camera.

The three kinds of SHARPNESS

In order to be considered perfectly sharp (although, occasionally, partial or total unsharpness may be desirable), a photograph must simultaneously possess three kinds of sharpness (compare the diagram on p. 57):

1. **Sharpness of focus**—sharpness in two dimensions—is a function of focusing: if the lens is correctly focused, the plane on which it is focused will appear sharp in the picture.

2. **Sharpness in depth**—sharpness in three dimensions—is a function of the diaphragm: the smaller the diaphragm aperture (the larger the *f*/stop number), the greater the extent of the sharply rendered zone in depth, and vice versa (more on p. 62).

3. **Sharpness of motion**—the absence of directional blur—is a function of the shutter speed: if the shutter speed is sufficiently high, a subject in motion will be rendered sharp; otherwise, it will appear more or less blurred (consult the table on p. 66).

If these three requirements are fulfilled, the photograph should be sharp in its entirety but may not, for one or several of the reasons discussed on p. 60.

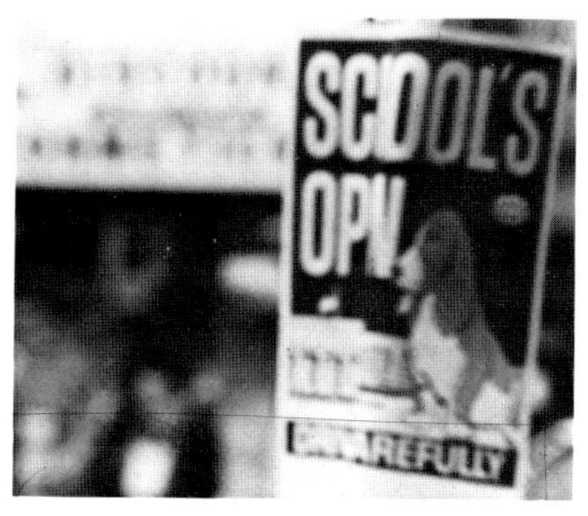

The four kinds of unsharpness

Overall, non-directional unsharpness (top, left) is the result of incorrect focusing.

Partial, non-directional unsharpness (top, right) is either the result of incorrect focusing, or insufficient stopping down of the diaphragm, or both.

Overall sharpness (right) is the result of correct focusing in conjunction with an appropriate diaphragm stop and shutter speed.

Partial, directional unsharpness (bottom, left) is the result of a shutter speed that was too low to "freeze" the movement of a subject in motion.

Overall, directional unsharpness (bottom, right) is the result of inadvertent camera movement during exposure.

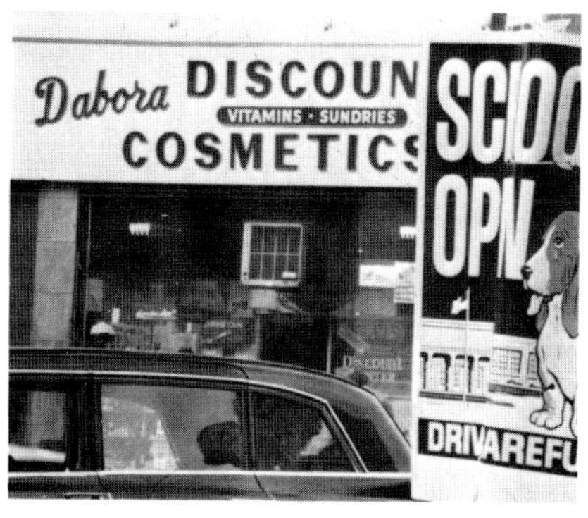

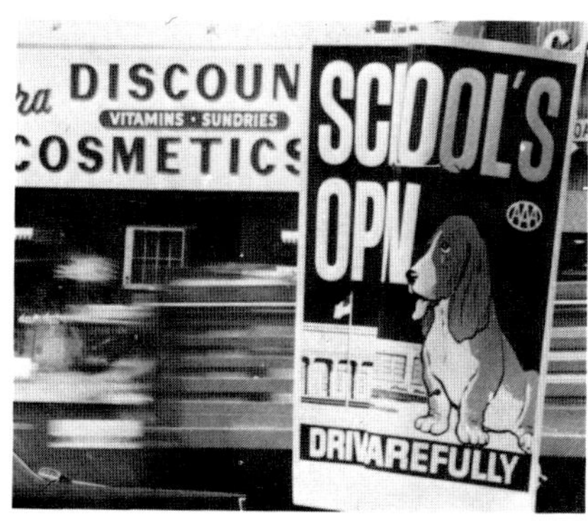

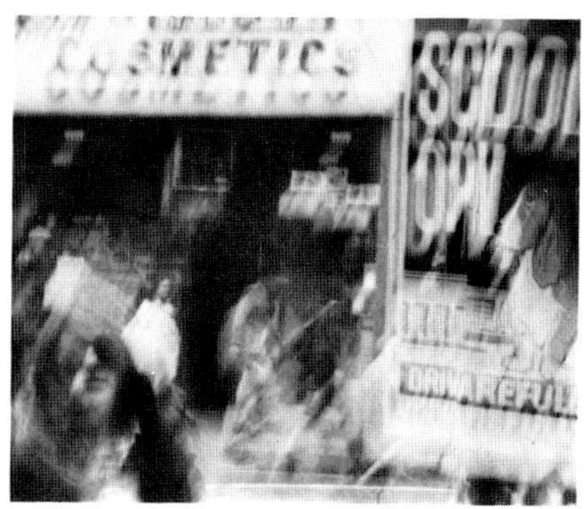

Common causes of **UNSHARPNESS**

Inadvertent camera movement during exposure is the most common cause of unsharp photographs; to avoid this danger, heed the following advice:

Don't use shutter speeds slower than 1/125 sec. unless the camera is firmly supported, either by a tripod or by pressing it hard against a rigid object like a wall, piece of furniture, automobile, lamp post, etc. When making hand-held shots, take a steady stance, feet slightly apart, upper arms tight against the chest. If possible, brace yourself further by leaning your shoulder, back, or hip against any support that might be handy. Get a comfortable grip on your camera and press camera and hands firmly against your forehead, nose, and cheek. Take a deep breath, let it out halfway, then hold it and make the exposure by rolling the tip of your index finger onto the shutter release button, gently "squeezing" it downward until the shutter goes off. Don't jab—this is a surefire way to jerk the camera at the precise instant it must be perfectly steady, the moment of exposure.

Mirror out of alignment or rangefinder out of synchronization. To check whether this is the case, make the test described on p. 35.

A dirty lens or filter. Fingerprints, greasy film, moisture condensation or raindrops on a lens or filter are common causes of unsharpness. To clean a lens or a glass-mounted filter, use a fine camel's hair brush to remove particles of dust and grit, then breathe on the glass and wipe it *lightly* (in order not to scratch an anti-reflex coating) with special lens-cleaning tissue, using a drop of lens-cleaning fluid if a more thorough cleaning job is required. Fingerprinted or scratched gelatin filters cannot be cleaned and should be replaced.

Focus shift of the lens. Focusing certain high-speed lenses wide open, then stopping down the diaphragm to take the picture, causes a slight degree of unsharpness because, at full aperture, the plane of focus is at a different distance from the lens than at smaller apertures. To yield sharp pictures, such lenses must be focused stopped down to shooting aperture.

Unsharp lens. Some lenses—like those of cheap box cameras, certain high-speed lenses at more or less full aperture, and all lenses in conjunction with a teleconverter (p. 44)—are inherently incapable of producing critically sharp pictures.

How to hold a camera steady during exposure

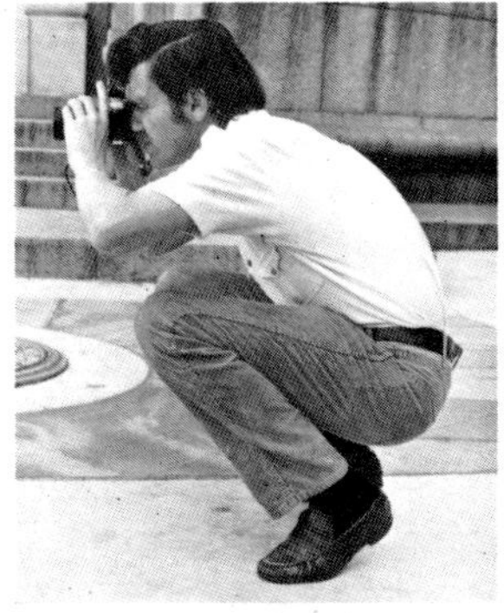

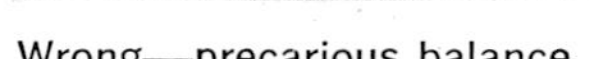

Wrong—precarious balance.

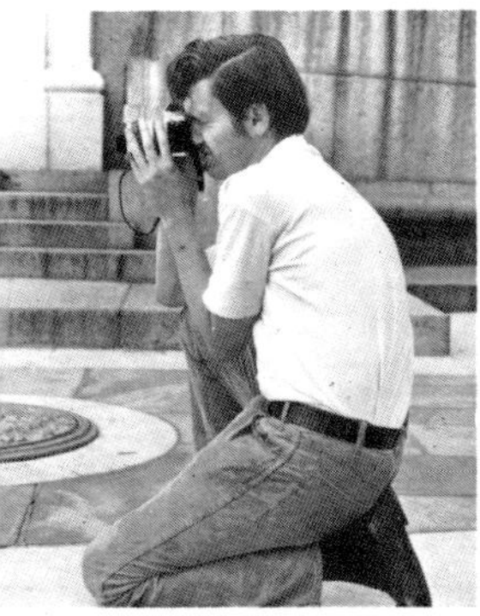

Correct—securely braced stances.

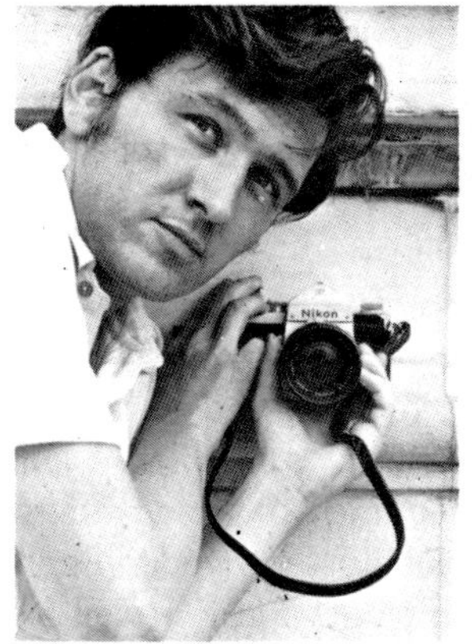

Camera pressed against a wall.

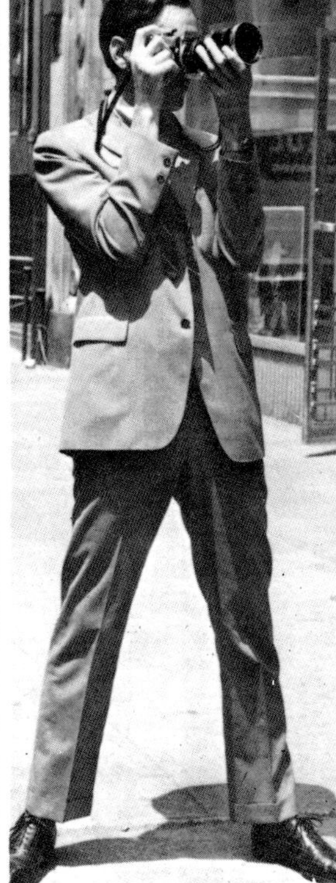

Well-braced standing position.

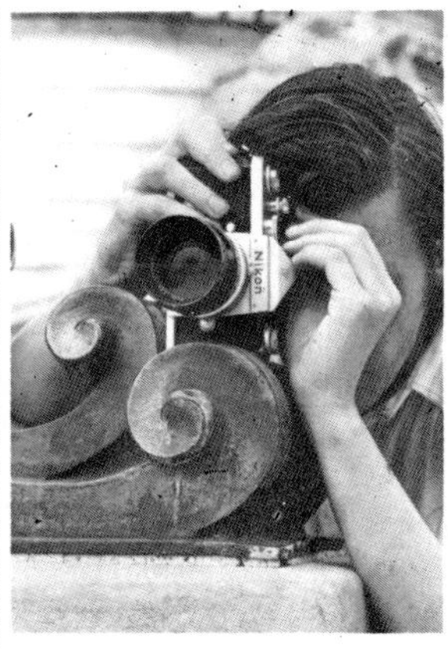

Camera firmly supported.

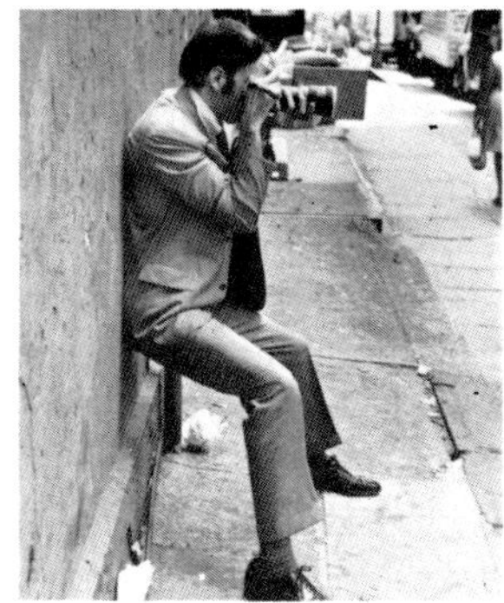

Back pressed against a wall.

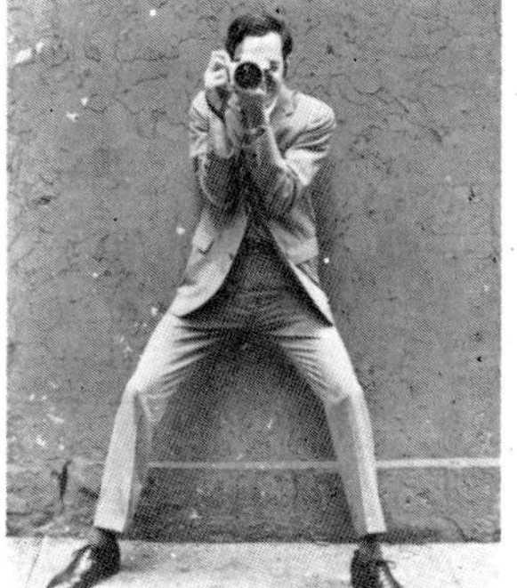

Well-braced position.

How to create **SHARPNESS IN DEPTH**

A lens can be focused only on a plane, but most photographic subjects are not flat, they are three-dimensional: in addition to height and width they have depth. This raises the question: how can a photographer convert two-dimensional sharpness into three-dimensional sharpness, *i.e.*, extend, in his picture, sharpness beyond the plane of focus in order to render his subject sharply in its entirety? The answer: by stopping down the diaphragm.

Stopping down the diaphragm has two effects upon the picture:

1. The smaller the diaphragm aperture (*i.e.*, the larger the *f*/stop number), the greater the depth of the sharply rendered zone (the depth of field), and vice versa.

2. The smaller the diaphragm aperture, the less light can reach the film in a given time, the darker the image and, other factors being equal, the longer the required exposure (*i.e.*, the lower the corresponding shutter speed), and vice versa.

This second, obviously disadvantageous effect makes it of course desirable to achieve maximum sharpness in depth with a minimum of stopping down. This is done by taking advantage of the following rule:

Stopping down the diaphragm increases sharpness in depth in two directions from the plane of focus: toward, and away from, the camera. However, sharpness in depth increases approximately twice as fast away from the plane of focus as toward the camera. Therefore, for maximum depth with minimum stopping down, the lens must be focused on a plane situated about one-third within the distance between the nearest and farthest parts of the subject that must be rendered sharply.

For example, in an interior photograph, if sharpness should begin 7 feet from the camera and extend 18 feet farther to the end of the room, the lens must be focused approximately at $7 + \left(\frac{18}{3}\right) = 13$ feet. The *f*/stop required to cover sharply this depth of 18 feet depends on the focal length of the lens and is most easily found with the aid of the depth-of-field calculator of the camera. Focus the lens until identical *f*/numbers appear on the calculator scale opposite the foot-numbers that correspond to the beginning and end of the depth zone that must be covered sharply (in this case, 7 and 25), then stop down accordingly. For more specific information, consult the instructions that came with your camera.

Stopping down the lens increases the extent of the sharply covered zone in depth: the smaller the diaphragm aperture (i.e., the larger the *f*/stop number), the greater the depth of the sharply rendered zone; and vice versa.

Of the photographs at the right, the top one was taken with the diaphragm wide open at *f*/2.8, and the one in the center with the diaphragm stopped down to *f*/32. In both cases, the lens was focused on the statue, which was located about one-third within the depth of the setup shown in the bottom picture.

This demonstration shows extremes: a very shallow and a very extensive zone of sharpness in depth. By using one of the intermediary *f*/stops, a photographer can, of course, render any intermediary depth zone sharply.

All-inclusive sharpness, however, is not always desirable. Occasionally, rendering the subject proper (here, the statue) sharp, and the foreground and background unsharp, can lead to better pictures.

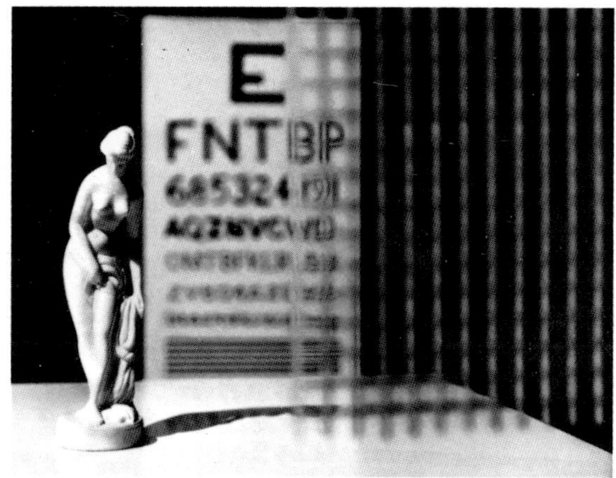

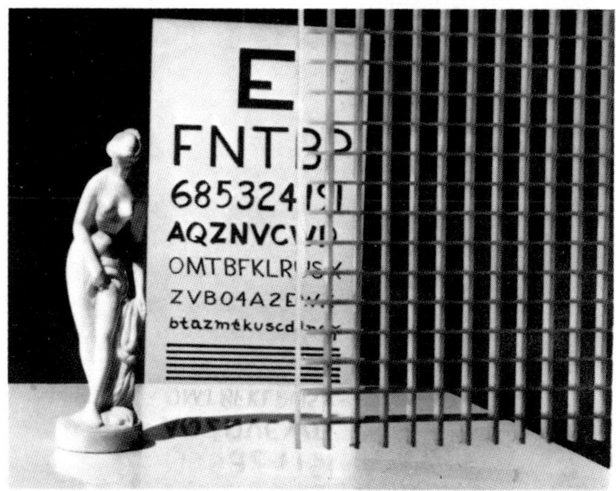

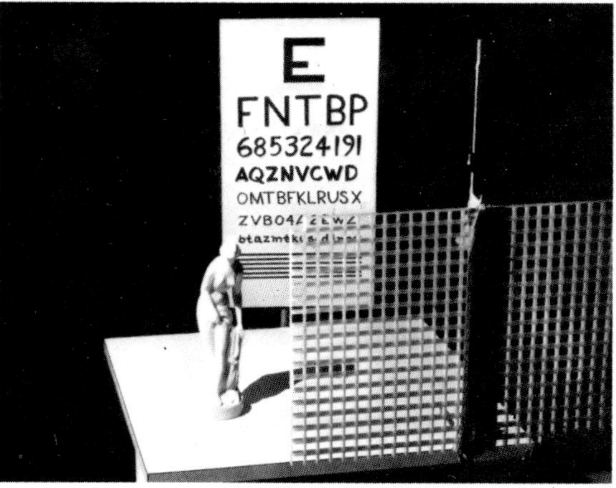

THE HYPERFOCAL DISTANCE

In cases in which it is necessary that sharpness in depth extend from a specific distance in front of the camera all the way to infinity, to create maximum sharpness with minimum stopping down, the lens must be focused on a plane located at what is called the *hyperfocal distance.* With the lens focused on the hyperfocal distance, a corresponding diaphragm stop then creates a zone of sharpness (depth of field) that extends from one-half the hyperfocal distance (measured from the camera) all the way to infinity. The following table gives the hyperfocal distances for a 35mm camera equipped with a two-inch (50mm) lens:

HYPERFOCAL-DISTANCE TABLE
for cameras with 2-in. (50mm) lenses

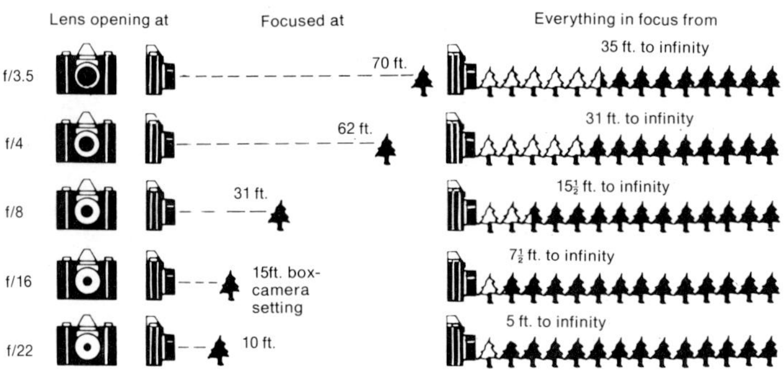

The hyperfocal distance for any lens of any focal length can be determined with the aid of the following formula in which F stands for the focal length of the lens in inches, f for the diaphragm-stop number, and d for the diameter of the so-called "circle of confusion" (permissible degree of unsharpness), which for 35mm cameras is 1/750 inch and for larger cameras equal to 1/1000 of the focal length of the lens that is standard for the respective format:

$$\text{hyperfocal distance (H)} = \frac{F^2}{f \times d}$$

To give an example: let's assume you wish to make a landscape photograph in which sharpness extends from the horizon (infinity) to as close to the camera as possible, using a 35mm camera equipped with a lens of two-inch focal length stopped down as far as possible which, in your case, should be $f/22$. You can then find the hyperfocal distance (H) with the aid of the following equation:

$$H = \frac{F^2}{f \times d} = \frac{2^2}{22 \times (1/750)} = \frac{4 \times 750}{22} = \frac{1500}{11} = 136 \text{ inches (approximately } 11\tfrac{1}{2} \text{ feet)}$$

Accordingly, by focusing your lens on 11½ feet and stopping down to $f/22$, you will be able to create a sharply rendered zone that extends from 5¾ feet (one-half the hyperfocal distance) all the way to infinity.

Conversely, if you wish to find the f/stop number that is required to render sharply any depth zone that extends from infinity to a given distance in front of the camera, use the following formula in which F stands for the focal length of the lens in inches, H for the hyperfocal distance in inches, and d for the diameter of the circle of confusion (for definition, see opposite page):

$$f/\text{stop number} = \frac{F^2}{H \times d}$$

For example, let's assume you wish to make a landscape photograph in which sharpness extends from the horizon (infinity) to 6 feet (one-half of the hyperfocal distance which, in this case, would then be $2 \times 6 = 12$ feet or 144 inches) from the camera, using a 35mm camera equipped with a lens of 2-inch focal length. You can find the required f/stop with the aid of the following equation:

$$f = \frac{F^2}{H \times d} = \frac{2^2}{144 \times (1/750)} = \frac{4 \times 750}{144} = \frac{3000}{144} = 20.8$$

Accordingly, by focusing your lens on 12 feet and stopping down to slightly less than $f/22$, you will be able to create a sharply rendered zone that extends from 6 feet in front of your camera (one-half the hyperfocal distance) all the way to infinity, a result that, incidentally, corresponds very nicely to our first example in which a hyperfocal distance of 11½ feet in conjunction with $f/22$ produced a depth of field extending from 5¾ feet to infinity.

And here is a suggestion for a rainy day: with the aid of the two formulas given here, compile a table of hyperfocal distances for all your lenses; it will prove invaluable whenever sharpness must extend from a certain distance in front of the camera all the way to infinity.

How to create sharpness of motion

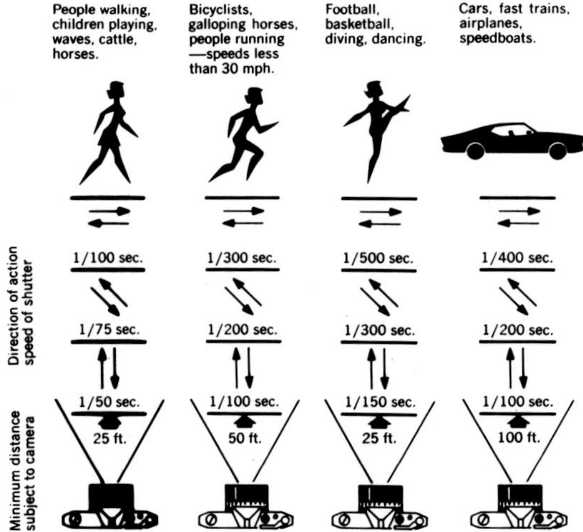

To render a subject in motion sharp, the photographer must use a sufficiently high shutter speed. In this respect, the faster the motion, the shorter the distance between moving subject and camera, and the more nearly at right angles to the optical axis the direction of the motion, the higher the shutter speed necessary to "freeze" the motion and render the moving subject in the form of a sharp picture.

The table at the left should give the reader an idea of the shutter speeds involved.

A SNAPSHOT SYSTEM

Settings for MEDIUM CLOSE-UPS			Film size and lens focal length (normal lens)	Settings for MAXIMUM DEPTH TO INFINITY (Hyperfocal distance)		
Aperture	Focus at	Depth		Aperture	Focus at	Depth
f/8	10 ft	7′8″ – 14′2″	35mm camera	f/8	30 ft	18′ –
f/11	15 ft	9′4″ – 39′	50mm lens	f/11	24 ft	12′ –
f/8	10 ft	8′4″ – 12′8″	2¼″ X 2¼″ camera	f/8	39 ft	19′ –
f/11	15 ft	10′4″ – 28′	80mm lens	f/11	28 ft	15′ –
f/8	10 ft	8′ – 13′	2¼″ X 3¼″ camera	f/8	41 ft	20′ –
f/11	15 ft	10′ – 30′	105mm lens	f/11	30 ft	15′ –

The interrelation between subject distance, focal length, and *f*/stop makes it possible to set the camera controls in such a way that a maximum of sharpness in depth is produced with a minimum of stopping down. Presetting his camera in accordance with the data given in the table above, a photographer can considerably increase his preparedness for unexpected events. Preselecting his shutter speed too (in accordance with the film speed, the *f*/stop used, and the ambient light), all he then has to do is aim the camera and shoot, assured that his subject will be in focus and his exposure right.

EXPOSING THE FILM

The purpose of exposing is to admit to the film the precise amount of light necessary to produce negatives with the right density and transparencies with colors that match those of the subject. Basically, the weaker the light and/or the slower the film (p. 23), the longer the exposure, and vice versa.

Determination of exposure should be based on the exposure table that is part of the instructions that accompany the film (which is sufficiently accurate for photographing average subjects under average light conditions) or, better still, the data established with the aid of a photoelectric exposure meter (p. 45) used in accordance with the instructions always accompanying it.

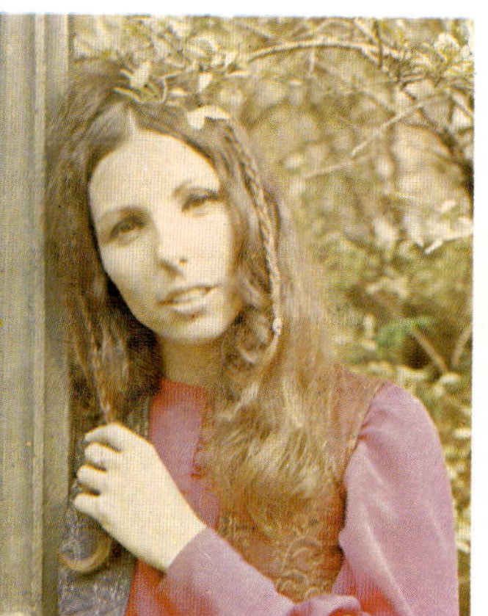

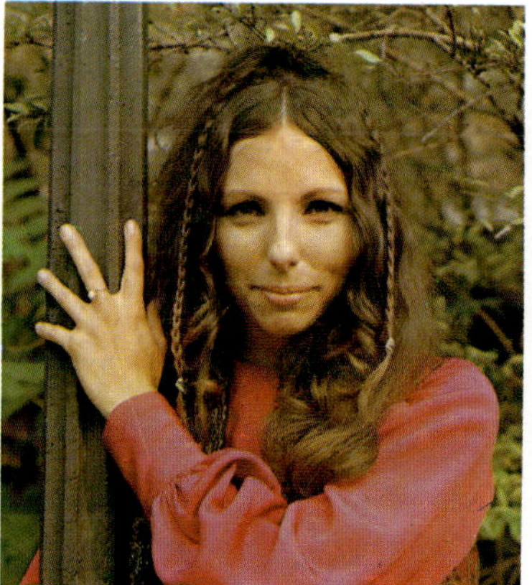

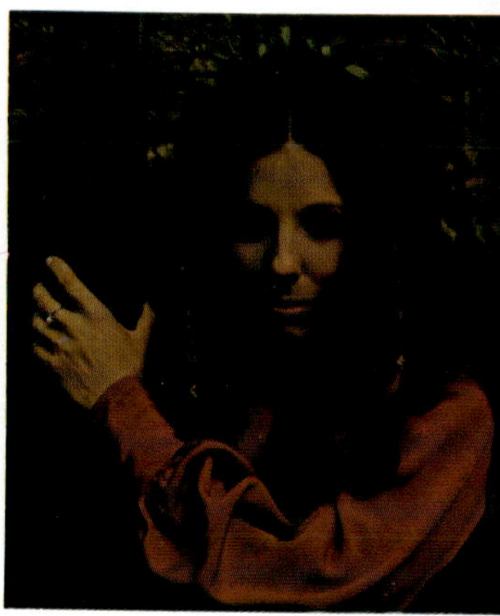

Overexposure results if the shutter speed is too low or the diaphragm aperture too large for the occasion. The colors of the transparency are then too light.

Correct exposure is the result of a diaphragm stop and shutter speed selected in accordance with the film speed and the brightness of the ambient light.

Underexposure results if the shutter speed is too high or the diaphragm aperture too small. The colors of the transparency will then appear too dark.

"Guessing" the exposure easily leads to failure because the human eye quickly and automatically adapts to small changes in brightness; as a result, we often are not even aware that such changes have taken place. Color film, however, acts promptly and strongly, yielding transparencies that are either over- or underexposed, as shown in the illustrations above.

Exposure regulation

Regulation of exposure is accomplished with the aid of two devices, each of which fulfills two functions:

the diaphragm controls	the volume of light admitted to the film the depth of the sharply rendered zone
the shutter controls	the time light is admitted to the film the sharpness of subjects in motion

Now, since a large diaphragm opening admits more light to the film than a small one and a high shutter speed admits less light to the film than a low one, it is obvious that, basically, as far as the exposure is concerned, a large diaphragm opening in conjunction with a high shutter speed accomplishes the same result as a small diaphragm opening in conjunction with a low shutter speed, or a medium *f*/stop in conjunction with a medium-fast shutter speed. Graphically, this can be expressed as follows:

The same amount of light is admitted to the film whether the exposure is, say, 1/500 sec. at *f*/1.8, 1/100 sec. at *f*/4, or 1/25 sec. at *f*/8. Therefore, as far as color rendition is concerned, the three transparencies would be identical, as proved by the pictures on the opposite page.

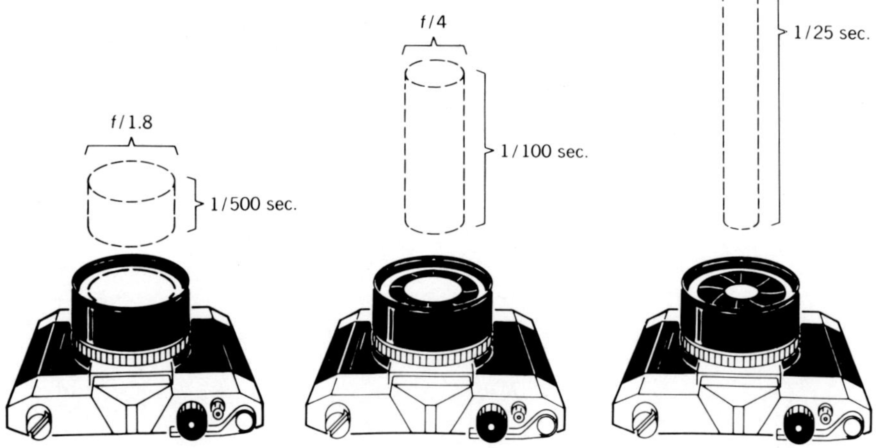

f/8
1/25 sec.
f/4
1/100 sec.
f/1.8
1/500 sec.

However, although transparencies produced by equivalent exposures are *identical in regard to color rendition*, they are *very different in regard to other important aspects,* specifically, in regard to the depth of the sharply rendered zone and the rendition of subject motion, as illustrated on the opposite page.

Exposure equivalents

One of the differences between a beginner and an experienced photographer is that the beginner knowing that a perfect exposure will result if he exposes, say 1/125 sec. at f/8 exposes accordingly, whereas an experienced photographer knows that 1/125 sec. at f/8 is only one of many different combinations of shutter speed and f/stop, each of which, under the same conditions, would yield a perfectly exposed color transparency. And in choosing the most appropriate combination of f/stop and shutter speed from the equivalents that he reads off the dial of his exposure meter, he would give careful consideration to the depth of his subject that has to be covered sharply (requiring a relatively small diaphragm stop) and possible subject motion (which might require a relatively high shutter speed). For he knows that photographic "know-how" leads to effective pictures only if guided by "know-why."

The accompanying pictures were shot at 1/1000 sec. at f/3.5, 1/100 sec. at f/11, and 1/25 sec. at f/22, respectively. Note the differences in sharpness in depth and rendition of motion.

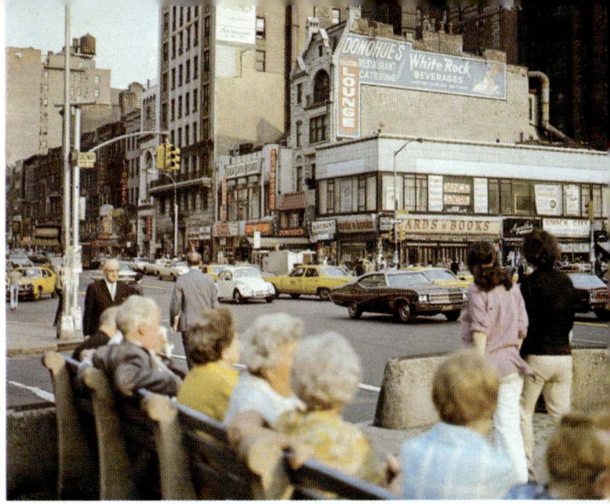

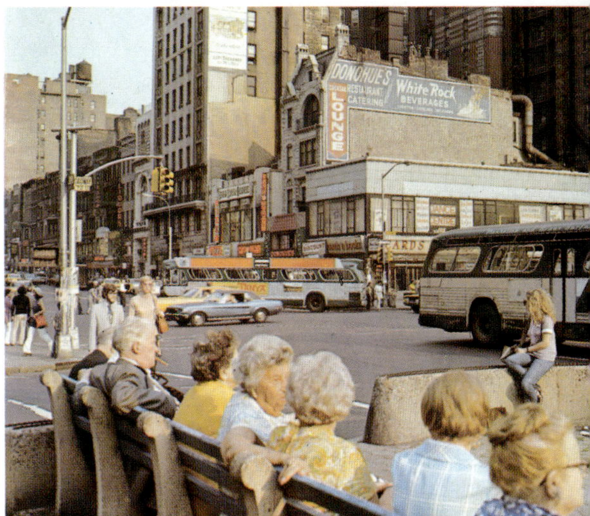

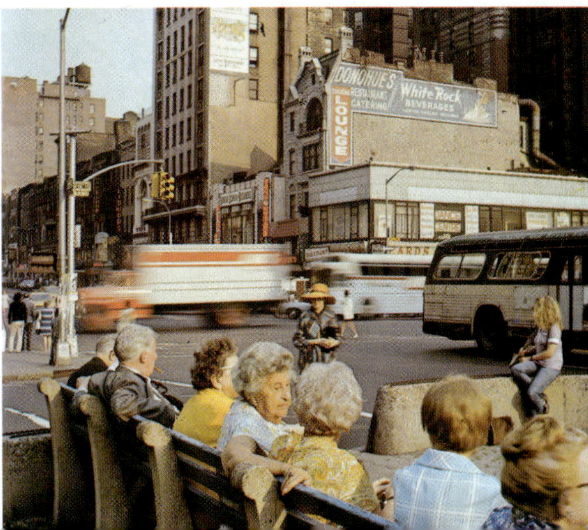

Exposure calculation

Calculation of exposure is best done with the aid of a photoelectric exposure meter (pp. 45–46) on the basis of the following equation:

$$\left.\begin{matrix}\text{film speed}\\ \text{brightness}\end{matrix}\right\} = \left\{\begin{matrix}f/\text{stop}\\ \text{shutter speed}\end{matrix}\right.$$

To take an exposure meter reading, set the film speed dial of the exposure meter (or camera) in accordance with the ASA speed number (p. 23) of the film you intend to use. Then measure the light reflected by the subject (if you use a reflected-light exposure meter) or the brightness of the light that illuminates your subject (if you use an incident-light exposure meter) in strict adherence to the instructions that came with your meter (or camera). The correctly set dial of your meter (or the pointer visible in the viewfinder of your camera) then gives you all the information you need for making a perfect exposure.

This information, however, although it contains everything you need to know, provides only the raw material for your calculation, which must be further refined in accordance with the specific requirements of the occasion; from the two dozen or more different combinations of *f*/stop and shutter speed indicated on the dial of your exposure meter, each of which would lead to a "perfect exposure," you must now choose the one combination that is most appropriate in your specific case. To be able to do this, you must, among other things, consider the following factors:

Should the picture be made with the *camera hand-held or firmly supported* (pp. 55, 60–61)? In the first case, to avoid blur through inadvertent camera movement during exposure, the shutter speed should be no less than 1/100 sec. and preferably higher, and the *f*/stop adjusted accordingly. In the second case you are, of course, free to choose any of the applicable shutter speeds.

How great is *the depth of your subject*—how extensive do you want the sharply rendered zone to be in depth? For the greater the extent of the sharply rendered zone in depth, the smaller the diaphragm aperture (the higher the *f*/stop number required); and the smaller the diaphragm aperture, the lower the corresponding shutter speed if underexposure is to be avoided.

But perhaps you wish to use the technique of *selective focus*, *i.e.*, keep the sharply rendered depth zone deliberately very shallow in order to symbolize "depth" through the juxtaposition of sharp and unsharp. If this is the case, you must work with a relatively large diaphragm opening, which, other factors being equal, requires the use of a correspondingly high shutter speed.

Is your *subject static or in motion*? In the first case, you can use any desired combination of *f*/stop and shutter speed because, if necessary, to avoid blur through inadvertent camera movement, you can always use a tripod or other firm camera support since your subject holds still. In the second case, you must make up your mind whether you wish to "freeze" subject motion or symbolize it through blur. Accordingly, you must either select a shutter speed high enough to "stop" motion on the film (see table on p. 66) or choose a shutter speed slow enough to cause blur but not too slow because, in that event, the moving subject might be rendered too blurred to remain recognizable in the picture. In either case, you would first have to select your shutter speed and then adjust the diaphragm aperture accordingly.

Do you wish to use a *filter or polarizer* to improve the color rendition in your picture (pp. 47–49, 87–91)? If so, the filter factor must be considered in accordance with the manufacturer's recommendations. For example, a factor of, say, 2× means that the diaphragm aperture must be doubled, *i.e.*, increased by one full stop, relative to the data furnished by the exposure meter; alternatively, the time of exposure can be doubled (for example, use 1/50 sec. instead of a meter-indicated 1/100 sec.). And if a color filter and a polarizer are used simultaneously, the factor of one must be multiplied by (NOT added to) the factor of the other, and the exposure must then be increased in accordance with this new combination factor.

In *close-up photography*, if the distance (D) between subject and lens is equivalent to, or shorter than, approximately eight times the focal length of the lens (F), to avoid underexposure, the exposure indicated by a hand-held exposure meter* must be increased by a factor that can be found with the aid of the following equation:

$$\frac{\text{lens-to-film distance} \times \text{lens-to-film distance}}{\text{focal length of lens} \times \text{focal length of lens}} \text{ or } \left(\frac{D}{F}\right)^2$$

*This does NOT apply to through-the-lens exposure meters built into the camera which, in this case, provide readings that automatically take the close-up factor into consideration.

For example, if you wish to make a close-up of a flower, using a 35mm camera equipped with a lens of two-inch focal length and auxiliary bellows, and, after focusing, the distance from lens center to film measures four inches, you can calculate the corresponding close-up factor with the aid of the following equation:

$$\left(\frac{D}{F}\right)^2 = \frac{4 \times 4}{2 \times 2} = \frac{16}{4} = 4$$

Accordingly, in order to avoid underexposure, you now must multiply the exposure determined with the aid of a hand-held exposure meter by four, *i.e.*, either open up the diaphragm two full stops or quadruple the time of exposure.

If exposure times are abnormally short (electronic flash) or long (time exposures), a complication called *reciprocity failure* may occur, which affects not only the exposure but often also the color rendition. The effects of reciprocity failure are unpredictable, vary with the respective film emulsion, and can be established only by tests. To aid the photographer in this task, Kodak includes pertinent information (if necessary) with all its color sheet films to which the reader is referred.

Some subjects cannot be "measured" by an exposure meter but must be exposed on the basis of data established empirically by tests. The following table provides such information:

SUBJECTS	TRIAL EXPOSURES		
	ASA 25	ASA 64	ASA 160
Brightly lit streets	8 sec. f/8	2 sec. f/5.6	1 sec. f/5.6
Electric signs (incl. Neon)	1 sec. f/11	1/2 sec. f/11	1/30 sec. f/4.5
Floodlit buildings	2 sec. f/8	1 sec. f/8	1 sec. f/11
Store windows	30 sec. f/8	15 sec. f/8	15 sec. f/11
Outdoor Christmas lights	16 sec. f/8	8 sec. f/8	4 sec. f/8
Christmas-tree lights (with fill-in flash)	1 sec. f/5.6-8	1 sec. f/11	1 sec. f/16
Outdoor fires, burning bldgs, etc.	1/10 sec. f/3.5 or 1 sec. f/11	1/10 sec. f/4.5 or 1 sec. f/16	1/10 sec. f/6.3 or 1 sec. f/22
Museum displays	30 sec. f/8	15 sec. f/8	15 sec. f/11
Circus or ice-show acts (spot-lit only)	1/25 sec. f/2	1/25 sec. f/2.8	1/25 sec. f/4
Star tracks at night (clear, dark night)	3 hrs. f/3.5	3 hrs. f/5.6	3 hrs. f/6.3

Incidentally, different shutters and different exposure meters may be calibrated differently. However, in practice, slight variations can safely be disregarded and the differences between, say, 1/100 and 1/125 sec., 1/50 and 1/60 sec., or 1/25 and 1/30 sec., ignored.

Bracketing

The number of variables that influence the color rendition—individual characteristics of the respective color film emulsion; spectral composition (color) of the ambient light; subject contrast; accuracy of shutter speeds; conditions under which the film was stored; manner of development; and personal preferences of the photographer in regard to transparency and color saturation—is so large that it is virtually impossible to predict precisely the outcome of the exposure. Therefore, if conditions permit, experienced photographers, in addition to the supposedly "correct" exposure, always make additional exposures of the same subject with slightly different f/stop settings (and sometimes different color filters as well), and, after development, pick the transparency they like best.

This method, called *bracketing*, has three advantages: it offers the photographer a choice of several transparencies that are subtly graded in regard to lightness (and/or overall color); it provides insurance in case of damage to or loss of the slide; and it results in two or more useable "originals" instead of only one (or, if that "one" exposure was incorrect, none).

To be effective, exposures must be spaced at half-stop intervals if positive color film is used and one full stop apart if negative color film is used. Smaller intervals would be wasteful; larger ones might cause the photographer to miss the best exposure.

A typical "bracket" of five different exposures spaced at half-stop intervals is shown in the test strip at the right.

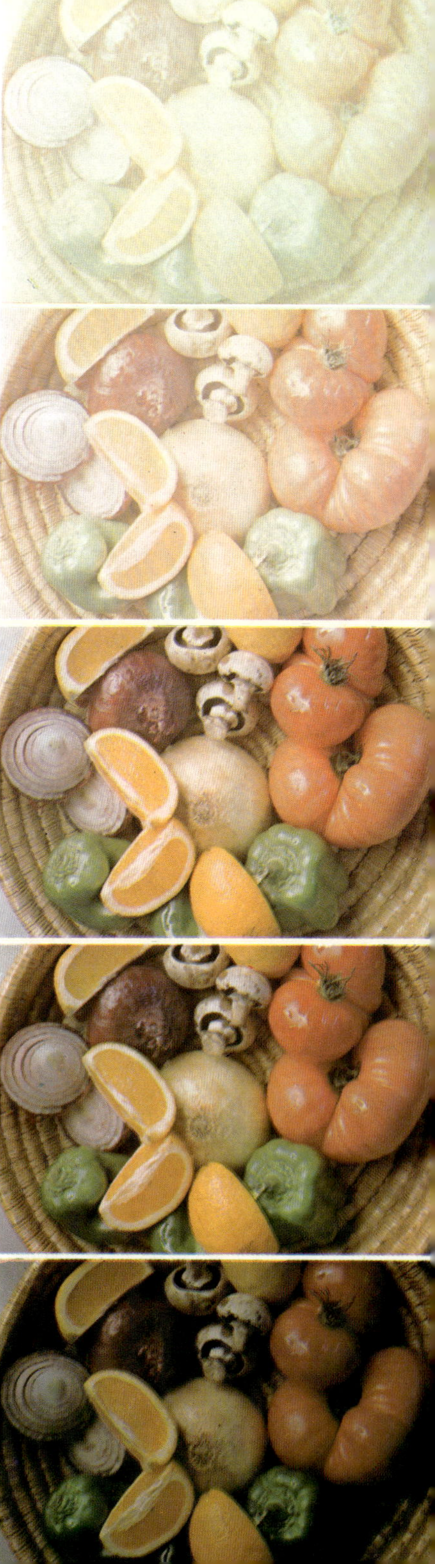

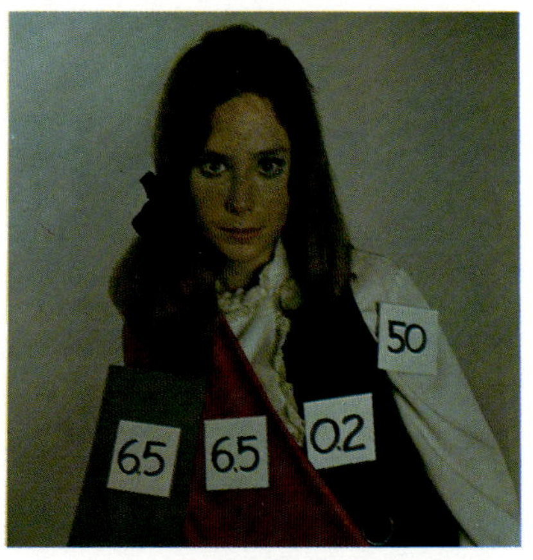

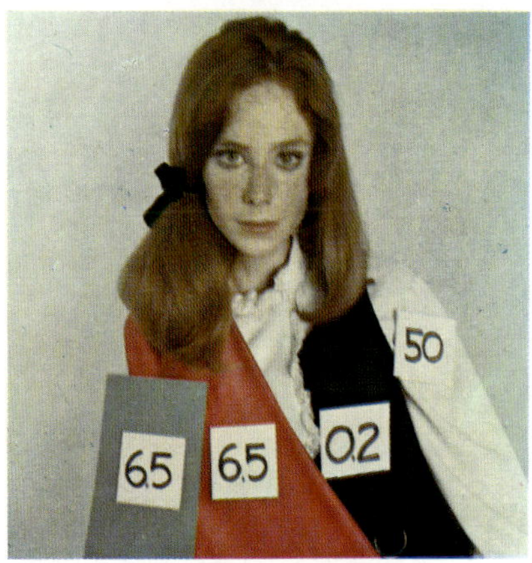

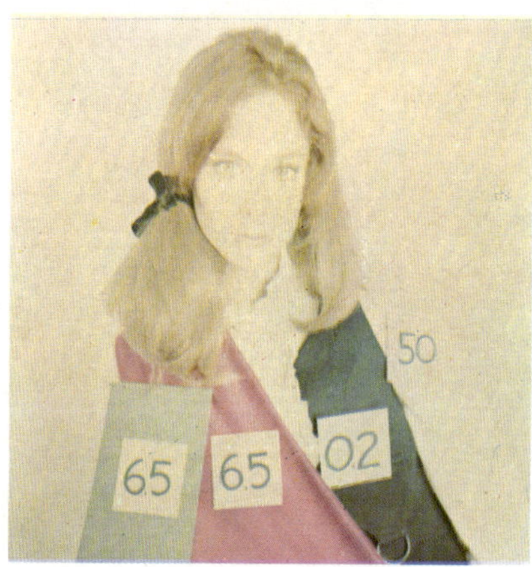

Exposure meters "think average"

Paradoxical as it may sound, it is a fact that by carefully measuring the brightness of the most important part of his subject (for example, a very pale face), a photographer may arrive at the wrong exposure. This is so because exposure meters are calibrated in such a way that a spot reading taken off any part of the subject, no matter whether light, medium, or dark, will lead to an exposure that renders the measured area as a medium-bright shade in the transparency.

The numbers in the pictures at the left represent brightness values established with the aid of a Weston exposure meter. The exposure of the picture at the top was based upon a reading taken off the lightest part of the subject (the white blouse); that of the center picture upon a reading taken off the gray Kodak Neutral Test Card, which represents a shade of "average brightness" (as does the bright red of the scarf); and that of the picture at the bottom upon a reading taken off the darkest part of the subject (the black cloth).

Not surprisingly, only the picture exposed in accordance with the reading taken off the "shade of average brightness" resulted in a picture in which the colors of the photograph correspond to those seen by the eye in reality, whereas the exposures based upon the carefully measured lightest and darkest shades resulted in underexposure and overexposure, respectively, with the "white" of the first and the "black" of the second appearing in almost identical shades of medium gray.

This characteristic of exposure meters to "think average" makes it imperative that a photographer using a spot meter or taking spot readings close-up with an integrating reflected-light meter select areas of "average" or medium brightness as the basis for calculating his exposures.

The influence of the SUBJECT CONTRAST

Satisfactory color rendition is possible only if the subject contrast does not exceed the contrast range of the color film which, for positive color film, is equivalent to two *f*/stops (brightness range 4:1) for *perfect*, and up to four *f*/stops (16:1) for *acceptable*, color rendition. For negative color film, the corresponding values are about twice as high. In other words for "perfect" color rendition, a meter reading taken off the darkest part of the subject must not indicate an exposure that is longer than four times as long (16 times as long for "acceptable" pictures) as a meter reading taken off its brightest parts.

Subject contrast is the product of two factors: the reflectance ratio and lighting ratio. **The reflectance ratio** of a subject is the difference in brightness between its lightest and darkest *colors* (*i.e.*, black and white, if present, are disregarded), provided all colors receive the identical amount of light. **Lighting ratio** is the difference in brightness between the subject areas that receive the most light and those that receive the least light, *i.e.*, the difference between the brightest highlight and the deepest shadow.

You can measure the reflectance ratio of your subject by taking close-up readings with a reflected-light exposure meter of its lightest and darkest *colors* (disregarding black and white, if present), first making sure that both receive *the same amount of light*. Outdoors, this will be the case if both are fully illuminated by the sun or both are equally shaded. Indoors, check the uniformity of the illumination with an incident-light meter; alternatively, hold a Kodak Neutral Test Card in front of the respective colors and measure their brightness with a reflected-light exposure meter—if you get identical readings with the card held in front of the lightest and darkest subject colors, both receive the same amount of light and your reflectance readings will be valid.

You can measure the lighting ratio of your subject either by measuring with a reflected-light meter the reflectance of a Kodak Neutral Test Card held in front of those subject areas that are fully illuminated and those that are in the deepest shade, respectively; or, by directly measuring with the aid of an incident-light exposure meter the brightness of the illuminating light source and that of the deepest shadow cast by it. Multiplying the reflectance ratio (say, 3:1) by the lighting ratio (say, 2½:1) then gives you the subject contrast ratio (in this case, 7½:1).

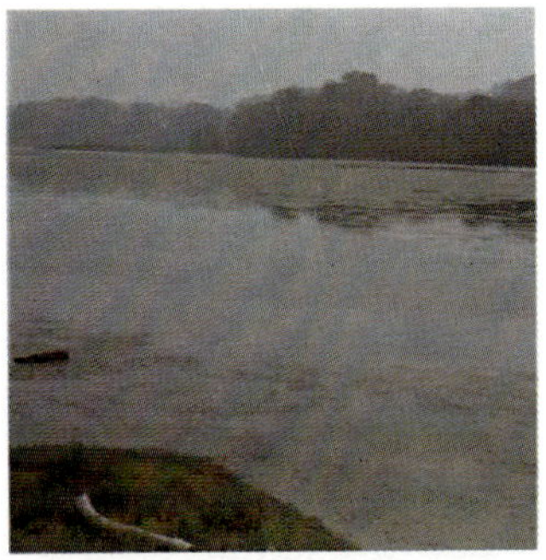

Exposure according to meter —scene appears too dark.

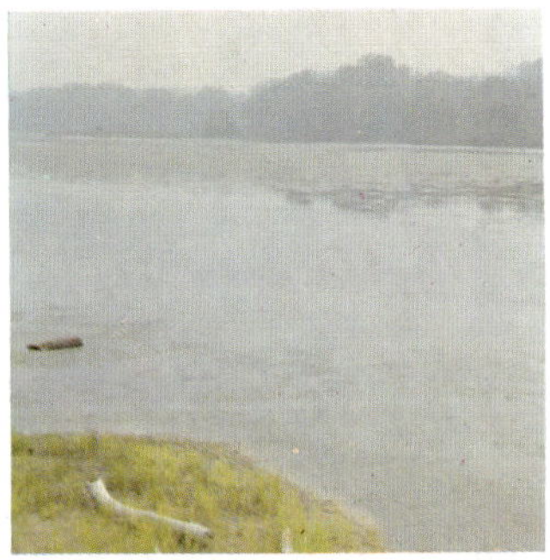

Exposure increased—brightness as it appears to the eye.

Low-contrast subjects

The scene above represents a *low-contrast subject of more than average brightness*. Exposed in accordance with a "straight" exposure meter reading (left), such a scene will be rendered *darker* than it actually is. Experienced photographers (and those who have read the explanation on the previous page) are aware of this and, when photographing *low-contrast subjects of more than average brightness* (like many snow, ice, beach, or fog scenes), *increase their exposure* by one-half to one and one-half *f*/stops. See picture above, right.

Conversely, *low-contrast subjects of less than average brightness,* if exposed in accordance with readings taken from an exposure meter, would be rendered *lighter* than they appear to the eye in reality. To avoid this, the *exposure must be shortened* by one-half to one and one-half *f*/stops. See pictures below: the one at the left was exposed according to the meter and appears too light; the one at the right, which received shorter exposure, matches the actual subject.

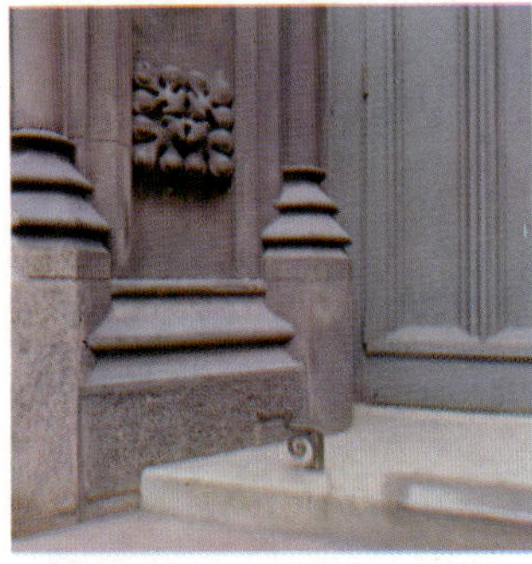

Exposure according to meter —subject appears too light.

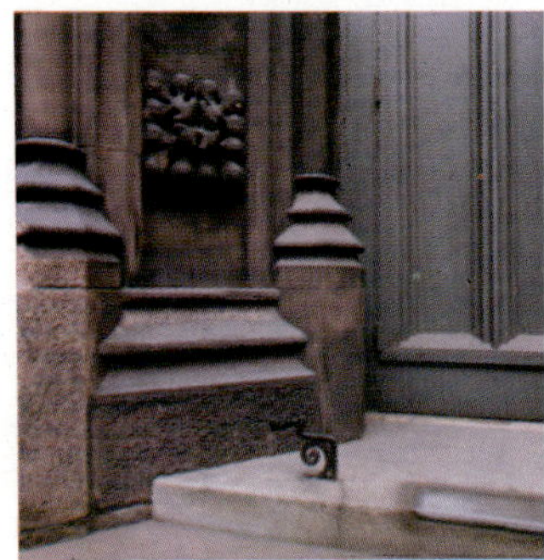

Exposure shortened—subject matches the actual scene.

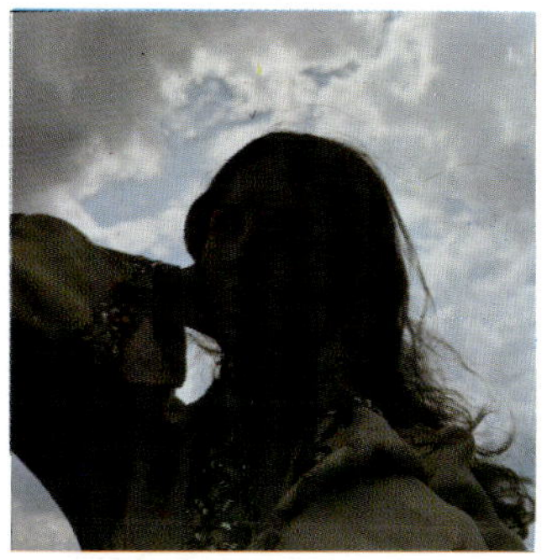

Exposed for the sky, the head appears too dark.

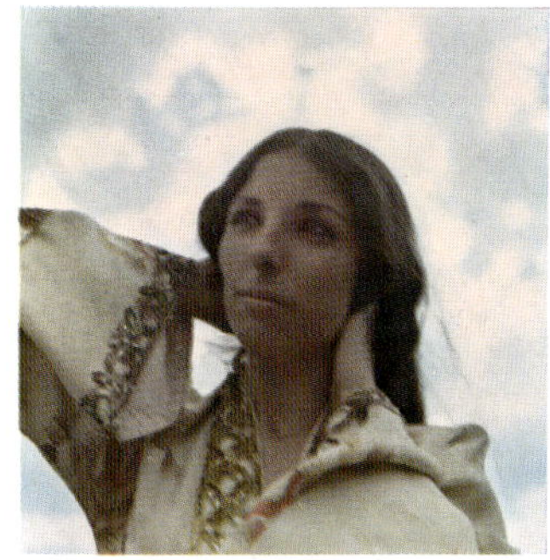

Exposed for the head, the sky appears too light.

High-contrast subjects

If subject contrast exceeds the contrast range of the color film, *only* the lightest, *or* the darkest, colors can be rendered correctly, but not both. In such cases, *selectively* exposing for the most important subject areas and letting the rest go either too dark or too light normally leads to better results than trying to "average" the exposure (as in the photograph at the right). Of the pictures above and below, the left ones were exposed for best rendition of their lightest areas and the right ones for their darkest. Subjects in which brightly lit and deeply shaded areas are equally important (picture at right) make notoriously disappointing photographs and should be avoided (unless contrast can be reduced; see pp. 98–101).

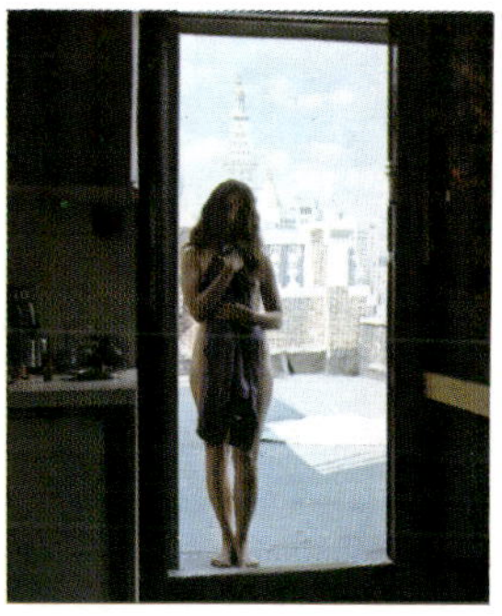

High-contrast scene, "averaged" exposure; over- and underexposure occur within the same picture.

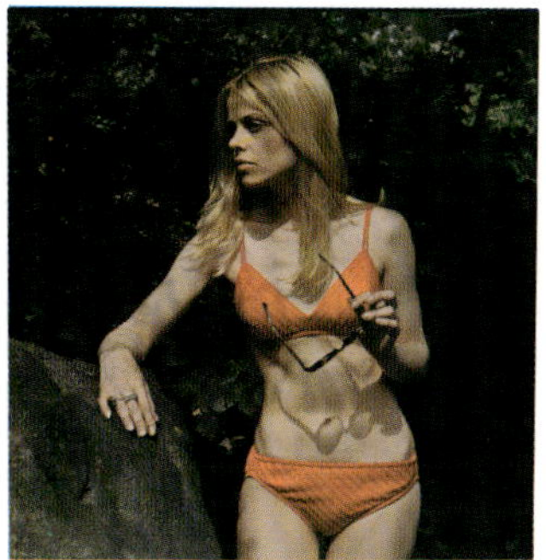

Exposure for skin tones leaves background too dark.

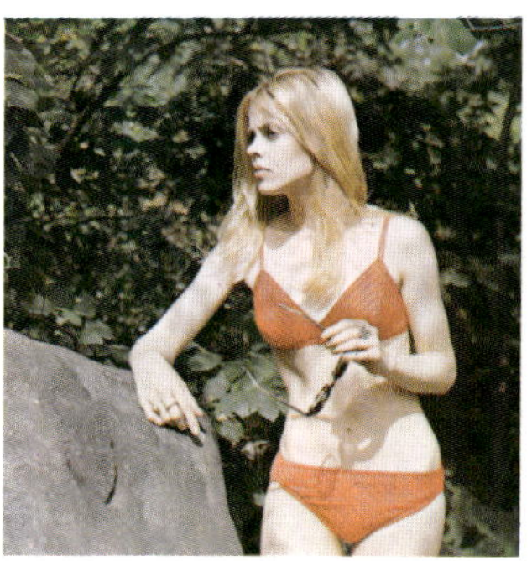

Exposure for background renders skin tones too light.

General advice and summary

Carefully read—and *study*—the instructions that accompany every new camera, exposure meter, speedlight, roll of film, etc. Collected and orderly filed, these booklets and data sheets form an impressive little reference library that is always authoritative—and it is free.

Photograph only subjects that genuinely interest you. Good pictures are made as much with the heart as with the camera. Unless you feel for your subject, you cannot convey feeling through your pictures to others. In this sense, interest in the subject is the vitally important catalyst without which communicative photographic work would be impossible.

Learn to distinguish between photogenic and unphotogenic subjects. Photogenic subjects have qualities like clarity, simplicity, spontaneity, unusualness, beautiful or significant coloration, etc., which make them particularly suitable to effective photographic presentation. On the other hand, unphotogenic subjects not only lack these qualities and therefore alone make notoriously disappointing pictures but are, in addition, disorganized, confused, abnormally contrasty, overloaded with unimportant detail, gaudy with a multiplicity of color, hackneyed in subject, and have been "done to death" by other photographers.

Right from the start, train yourself to avoid the two most common photographic faults: shooting from too far away or with a lens of insufficient focal length (this leads to pictures in which the subject proper appears too small to be effective; see also pp. 26–29) and inadvertently moving the camera during the exposure (this causes the picture to be blurred; see also pp. 60–61).

Pay attention to the background against which you show your subject. It should be subordinate to the subject yet set it off effectively, *i.e.*, it must be sufficiently different in color and texture so that subject and background do not blend. Outdoors, particularly unsightly and normally to be avoided are telephone wires or power lines crossing the sky, utility poles, wire fences, disturbing trees or branches, and patches of bright sky glaring through dark foliage. Indoors, when working with artificial light, avoid ugly shadows cast on a wall, wallpaper or drapes with confusing patterns, and gaudy fabrics or papers as backgrounds for small objects.

Watch the direction of the incident light relative to your subject. Front light—light coming over your shoulder as you face the subject—is most conducive to faithful color rendition; sidelight improves the feeling of "depth" in a picture; backlight—light shining toward the camera—is potentially the most effective and always the most risky type of light (see also pp. 96–97).

Never load your camera in direct sunlight or your film may accidentally be fogged. If there is no shade, turn away from the light and load the camera in the shadow cast by your body.

Make sure your camera is loaded with the right type of color film: positive color film for transparencies and slides for projection; negative color film for color paper prints; daylight type, Type A, or Type B color film in accordance with the kind of light in which you are going to photograph (see also pp. 22–24).

To remember the type and ASA speed of the film with which your camera is loaded, tear the square top off the end of the film wrapper and tape it to your camera as a constant reminder. But don't forget to change it the next time you load another type of film.

When using a 35mm camera, make sure the film is advancing properly by watching the rewind knob: if it turns as you wind the film, everything is in order; if it does not, the film does not advance because it has slipped out of the takeup spool or torn its perforation.

Unless other considerations make it undesirable, shoot at the highest practical shutter speed to avoid blur due to movement of the subject or the camera during the exposure. The slight gain in lens definition derived from the use of a smaller *f*/stop is usually not worth risking a blurred picture due to insufficiently high shutter speed.

When working with a 35mm rangefinder camera, don't forget to remove the lens cap before shooting.

Don't forget to set the frame counter back to zero after loading your camera unless, of course, your camera does this automatically.

And finally—remember what I said on p. 25 about handling film.

DEVELOPING AND PRINTING

Color film development involves processes that are considerably more complicated, critical, and, as far as equipment and material are concerned, expensive than those required for processing black-and-white films. Ektachrome film development (Process E-4), for example, involves 13 different steps, including two separate developing operations, which require that the temperatures of the solutions be maintained within plus or minus ½°F and ¼°F, respectively. And developing a single roll of film takes 49 minutes.

Printing color negatives, too, is considerably more complex than printing black-and-white films. For consistently good, repeatable results, the darkroom should be air-conditioned, solutions temperature-controlled, the enlarger color-balanced and voltage-stabilized, the color negatives color-analyzed electronically, and the print color-filtered and dodged. I realize—and amateur photo magazines love to report on this--that quite a number of amateurs develop their own color films and make their own prints, apparently overcoming all technical obstacles with Yankee ingenuity and simple, inexpensive means. Actually, however, things are slightly different. Either the means are not quite as simple as alleged, or the results, although pleasing enough as far as their proud producers are concerned, are not exactly what is popularly called up to snuff.

It is partly for these reasons that I feel that explicit instructions for color film development and printing are beyond the scope of this little guide. But my main reasons are that Kodachrome films, the favorite color material for 35mm slides, require automatic machine development, which is provided *only* by commercial color labs or the Eastman Kodak Company; that the majority of amateur photographers who will follow this guide use positive color films that don't require printing; that competent color services are available to anyone, if not directly, then by mail (consult the ads in the photo magazines); and, especially, that explicit and authoritative instructions for use accompany every color processing kit, whereas instructions given here might already be obsolete and superseded by new ones by the time this book appears in print. And finally, for developing and printing Kodak color films, the reader will find a veritable gold mine of information in the inexpensive Kodak Color Data Books, which, in my opinion, are indispensable to anyone intending to develop or print his own Kodak color films.

III. The Art of Color Photography

Excessive concern with the means of photography—the fascination of handling fine precision instruments, discussions on the merits of the various "system cameras," testing lenses for sharpness and films for graininess and color response, etc.—can turn the interest of the student photographer in a direction that leads to a dead end: technical perfection as the measure by which to judge the value of a photograph. In their eagerness to become proficient in the techniques of photography such people forget that, as in any other field, in photography, too, technique is only a means to an end—the end, in this case, being communication. They forget that very few photographers make pictures solely to please themselves but wish to have them seen and appreciated by people whom they want to inform, entertain, convince, or impress. However, whereas most people will gladly pay attention to, and even be impressed by, pictures showing interesting subjects effectively presented, only hidebound photographers are impressed by pointless "technique." In other words, unless a photograph has purpose and meaning, is interesting in regard to subject matter and well composed, not even the most accomplished "technique" can make it "good."

The opposite approach to photography—using the camera as a means of self-expression and the heck with "technique"—is equally self-defeating because the observer of the picture usually cannot understand what it is all about; lack of adequate "technique" turns the intended "communication" into visual gibberish.

Therefore, since the goal of any ambitious photographer is to make "good" pictures, it seems to me his first concern should be to find out what the elusive something is that makes a photograph "good." According to my experience, whether a photograph is good, bad, or indifferent depends entirely on the degree to which the photographer succeeded in solving the problem of making a picture in regard to three decisive aspects: *content* (the kind of subject and its meaning), *form* (the way in which the subject is "seen"), and *execution* (the way in which the subject is graphically presented). To be able to arrive at a satisfactory solution, he must ask himself and answer two questions:

What do I wish my picture to say?
How can I say it most effectively?

What do you wish your picture to say?

The "what" determines the content of your future picture—*the kind of subject* you wish to photograph, the *subject qualities* you wish to emphasize, and *the feeling about your subject* you wish to communicate through your picture. However, before you can communicate feelings, you have to feel something yourself, which means reaction, involvement, *interest*. Interest, therefore, is the prime factor without which no "good" photograph can be made.

The conclusions are obvious: photograph only subjects in which you are genuinely interested (professional photographers, of course, may not have this choice, this priceless privilege of the amateur). In particular, it means don't imitate: don't do what others have done successfully before merely because you think that what worked for them will also work for you, no matter how different your personalities and interests, equipment and techniques. Because, once you have fallen into the trap of imitation, as far as your creative potential is concerned—your development as a photographer in your own right—you are dead.

Interest is the energizing factor that fuels every form of creative activity. Without being interested in his subject, a photographer cannot instill that element of excitement in his work which alone can stir the imagination of the viewer of the picture and arouse *his* interest—and a photograph that doesn't arouse interest is worthless, no matter how technically accomplished its execution.

As long as you are truly interested in your subject it doesn't matter *what* you photograph—whether girls or garter snakes, people, places, or postage stamps—because no one is unique in that he cannot find other people to share his interests. And neither does it matter *how* you photograph the subject that interests you, as long as you express in your own way your feelings and the subject qualities that caught your interest. If this comes out in your pictures—excitement, compassion, opinion, an individual reaction, a personal way of seeing things—others may still not agree with you, but no one can question your integrity as a photographer, and your statements will be valid.

How can you express yourself most effectively?

Before a photograph can be appreciated, it must be noticed. Unfortunately, the massive flood of images in newspapers, magazines, advertisements, books, on TV tubes and movies screens, etc., has satiated most people to such a degree that they notice only those pictures that are outstanding or unusual. Therefore, the first requirement of any "good" photograph is visual stopping power.

Stopping power, which plays the role of a flashing light, a device to attract attention, can be generated by anything that makes a picture graphically conspicuous, like strikingly bold or pale sophisticated color, perspective distortion, unusual composition, the "monumental" effect of a super-telephoto perspective, flare and halation, etc.

However, by itself, stopping power is insufficient to make a picture "good" and, unless applied in accordance with the characteristics of the subject, can easily degenerate into trickery. Much more is needed—a way of "seeing" that enables the photographer to render the special qualities of his subject in the graphically most effective form. This he does by making use of his *privilege of choice*: choice of the most suitable camera type or size, the most suitable lens, the most suitable filter, film, type and color of light, or direction of the illumination; choice of rectilinear, cylindrical, or spherical perspective; choice of focal length in conjunction with subject distance for most appropriate scale and perspective; choice of type of foreground, background, weather, clouds and sky. The possible variations and combinations are unlimited, their scope defined only by the scope of the imagination of the photographer, who thereby can present any given subject in any one of countless different forms. Some of the means by which he can achieve his goal are discussed on the following pages.

By experimenting with these means in meaningful combinations a photographer creates new forms of expression—purposeful violation of antiquated "rules" is a prerequisite for progress. And if the form of presentation that a photographer deems most suitable for the characterization of his subject—no matter whether this form is "old" or "new"—is executed in accordance with the precepts of modern phototechnology, the circle is complete and the photograph will be good; reality has been transformed into art.

THE QUALITIES, TYPES, AND FUNCTIONS OF LIGHT

Experienced color photographers realize that light is one of the main factors that decide the appearance of a picture. They know that it makes a great difference whether they shoot, for example, outdoors at noon or early or late in the day; with front-, side-, or backlight; in full sunlight, in the open shade, or under an overcast sky, and so on. Consequently, they pay a great deal of attention to the light that illuminates their subjects which, as far as they are concerned, has four main qualities:

Brightness (pp. 67–73)
Color (pp. 86–93, 106–115)
Direction (pp. 96–97)
Contrast (pp. 74–77, 98–99)

In addition, they distinguish between four main types of light:

Direct light (pp. 50–52, 96–97)
Diffused light (pp. 54, 100–103)
Reflected light (p. 98)
Filtered light (pp. 47–49, 87–91)

For practical reasons, they differentiate between

Natural light (pp. 86–93)
Artificial light (pp. 100–105)

Finally, they utilize the three main functions of light which are:

Illuminating the subject
Symbolizing volume and depth
Setting the mood of the picture

Brightness is the measure of the intensity of light and can be measured with an exposure meter (pp. 45–46, 74–77). Brightness determines the exposure, indicates whether the camera can be hand-held or must be more firmly supported (pp. 60–61, 70), and influences the mood of the picture.

The color of the light determines which type of color film must be used (pp. 24, 94–95), whether or not a filter is required (pp. 47–49, 87–89), and the overall color shade of the picture. More on pp. 86–93, 106–115.

The direction of the incident light determines the position and extent of the shadows. In this respect, distinguish between front light, sidelight, backlight, top light, and light from below, about which more will be said on pp. 96–97.

Contrast between light and shadow determines whether or not the lightest and darkest colors of the subject can be rendered satisfactorily together. More on pp. 74–77, 98–99.

Direct light is contrasty, casts strong and well-defined shadows, and has a specific color temperature (p. 86), which can be measured with a color temperature meter. Typical sources are the sun, a spotlight, a photoflood lamp, flash (pp. 50–54).

Diffused light—direct light modified by a diffuser, light from an overcast sky—is relatively soft, less contrasty than direct light, and particularly well suited as shadow fill-in light. More on pp. 54, 100–103.

Reflected light is very soft, casts only weak and vaguely defined shadows, and has no color temperature in the true meaning of the term. Its color is a mixture of the color of the incident light and that of the reflecting surface. Typical sources: the blue sky and "bounce light," *i.e.*, flash illumination reflected from a ceiling or a wall. More on pp. 92–93, 98.

Filtered light has lost part of its spectrum—the colors absorbed by the filter through which it passed. Accordingly, photographs taken in filtered light (tinted window glass, colored gelatins in front of the lens or photo lamps) show an overall cast in the color of the filter. More on pp. 47–49, 87–91.

Natural light—the different forms of daylight—is unpredictable, ever changing not only in regard to brightness (which is easily determined with an exposure meter, see pp. 67–77) but also in regard to color: now "white," now yellow, reddish, purplish, or blue. More on pp. 86–93.

Artificial light is both predictable and constant in regard to brightness and color and therefore particularly suitable for color photography. More on pp. 100–105.

The concept of COLOR TEMPERATURE and its application

If we heat a piece of iron in a gas flame, it eventually becomes hot enough to emit light, first in the form of a dull reddish glow, then bright cherry-red. And as the temperature rises—for example, in a blast furnace—the light radiated by the incandescent metal changes in color from red to orange to yellow to white. A fixed relationship exists between the temperature of a radiant body (such as molten steel, the sun, or the filament of a photo lamp) and the color of the light it emits; the color of radiant light can be defined in terms of temperature.

The unit of color temperature measurement is the degree Kelvin. Its scale is the Kelvin scale, which starts at —273° C (absolute zero). Thus, the reddish light of a piece of iron heated to 1000° C has a color temperature of 1273 K. The following survey lists the approximate color temperatures or their equivalents of some light sources commonly used in photography:

Light Source	Color temperature	Decamired value
100-watt general-purpose lamp	2850	35
500-watt professional tungsten lamp	3200	31
500-watt amateur photoflood lamp	3400	29
500-watt blue photoflood lamp	4800–5400	21–19
blue-lacquered flashbulb	6000	17
electronic flash	6200–6800	16–15
morning and afternoon sunlight	5000–5500	19
sunlight through thin overall haze	5700–5900	18
noon sun, blue sky, white clouds	6200	16
light from a totally overcast sky	6700–7000	15
light from a hazy or smoky sky	7500–8400	12
blue skylight only, subject in the shade	10,000–12,000	9
clear blue northern skylight	15,000–27,000	6–4

The beauty of defining the color of the incident light in terms of color temperature is that it provides a practical solution to the problem of determining the appropriate filter, which, in effect, permits a photographer to convert a "wrong" type of light into the kind of light for which his color film is "balanced" (in the "wrong" light, color rendition would be "unnatural"). The key to this operation is a function of the color temperature, the so-called "decamired value," which for different types of *light* is listed in the table on the opposite page and for different kinds of *color films* below:

Daylight-type color films	16
Type A color films	29
Type B color films	31

Light-balancing filters in turn possess specific decamired conversion factors, which, together with their exposure-increase factors, are listed below for Kodak Filters Series 81 and 82:

Kodak Filter		Approximate conversion power in decamireds (Precise values in parentheses)	Exposure increases in f/stops (approx.)
reddish	81	1	1/3
	81A	2 (1.8)	1/3
	81B	3 (2.7)	1/3
	81C	3.5	1/2
	81D	4 (4.2)	2/3
	81E	4¾	2/3
	81EF	6	2/3
	81G	6½	1
blue	82	1	1/3
	82A	2	1/3
	82B	3	2/3
	82C	5	2/3
	82C + 82	6	1
	82C + 82A	7	1
	82C + 82B	8	1–1/3
	82C + 82C	9	1–1/3

To find the appropriate light-balancing filter, find the decamired values for the type of light by which you work (see list on opposite page) and for the color film you intend to use (see list at the top of this page), then subtract the smaller value from the larger. Let's assume the difference is 5. Now, if the *light* has a *higher* decamired value than the color film, you need a *blue* filter of conversion power 5 (82C); conversely, if the *film* has the *higher* decamired value, you need a *reddish* filter of conversion power 5 (81E). If the decamired values for light and film are the same, you don't need any filter at all. And at home, where you have access to this book, you can find the required filter simply by consulting a chart—the Nomograph on p. 49.

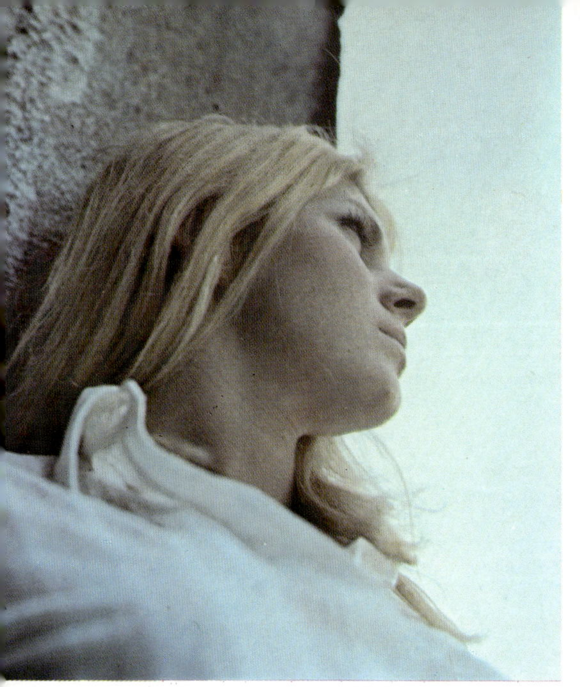

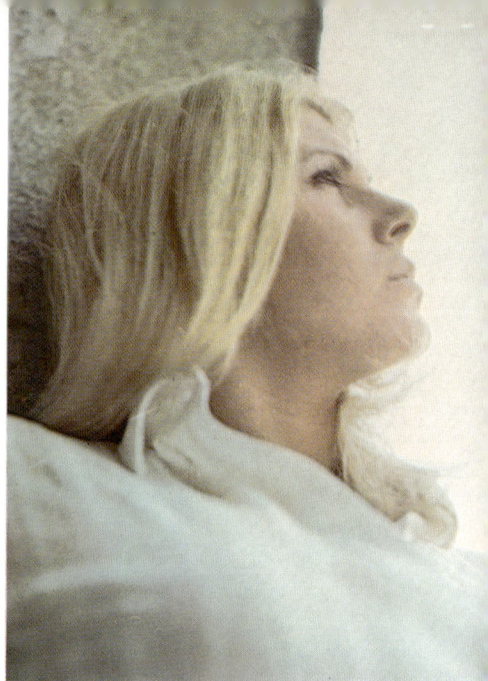

Outdoor portrait shot on daylight film in the open shade, with the face illuminated by blue skylight only. Left: no filter used, face appears bluish. Right: use of an 81G filter (p. 87) enabled the photographer to render the face in "normal" tones despite the strong blue tinge of the ambient light.

Color control through FILTERS

As I said before, natural-appearing color rendition can be expected only if the incident light matches the light for which the color film is "balanced." If this is not the case, the colors of the transparency will not match the colors of the subject as they appear to the eye in standard ("white") daylight (p. 92). In reddish sunset light, for example, a face can look lobster red to the eye and, without a blue correction filter, would be rendered thus in the transparency. But although the eye perceives the face as red, the mind subconsciously corrects for this abnormal redness and "remembers" the color of the face as it "normally" appears, *i.e.*, in "white" daylight—the transparency will be rejected as "unnatural."

Whether a photographer wishes to make creative use of such "unusual" colors or "correct" them with the aid of filters is, of course, entirely up to him. The accompanying picture pairs illustrate what can be done in this respect.

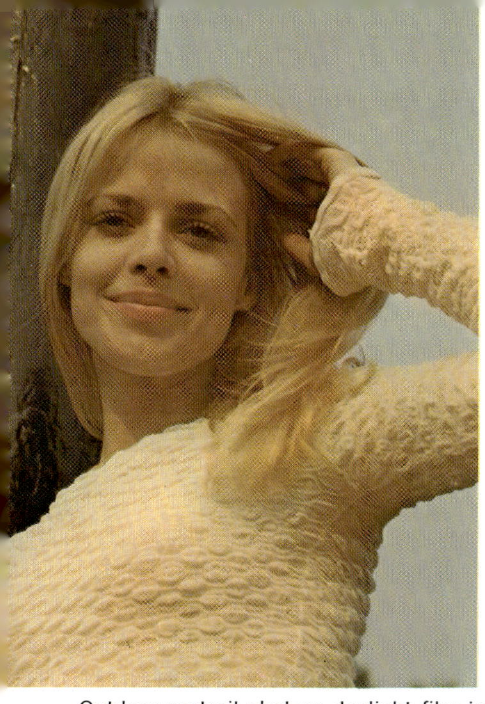

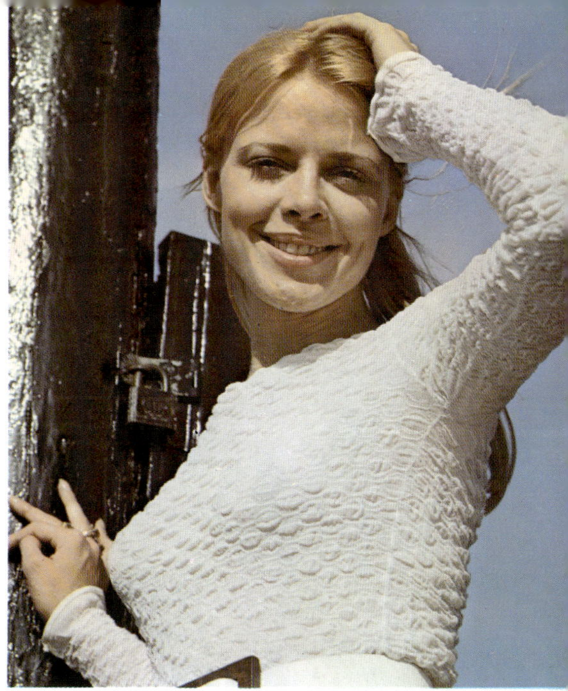

Outdoor portrait shot on daylight film in the late afternoon. Left: No filter used, face appears too reddish. Right: Use of an 82C filter (p. 87) enabled the photographer to render the face in "normal" skin tones and the actually white sweater as white.

Indoor portrait shot by incandescent light on Type B color film. Left: Illumination provided by a 100-watt household bulb, all colors are distorted toward yellow. Right: Use of an 82A filter, converting the light to "standard" as far as the film is concerned, resulted in "natural" appearing color.

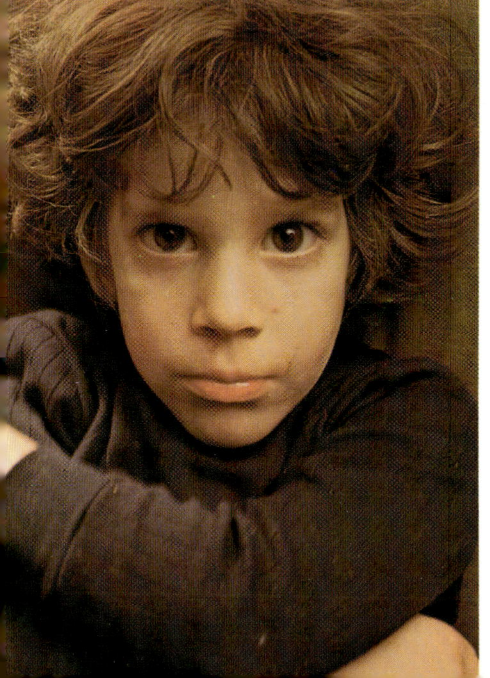

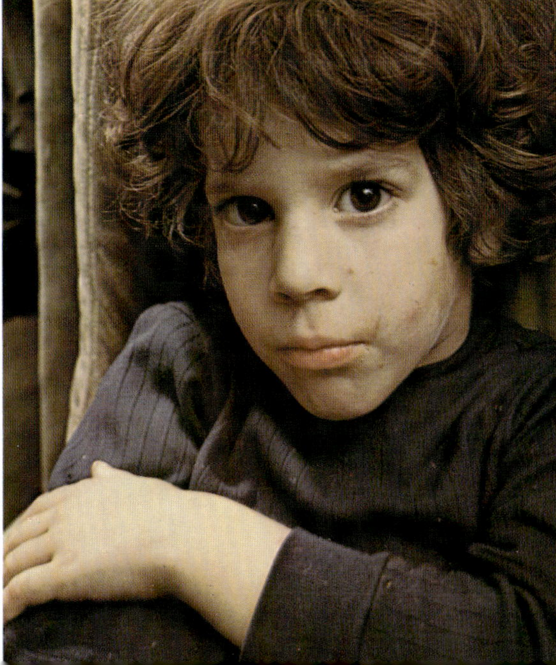

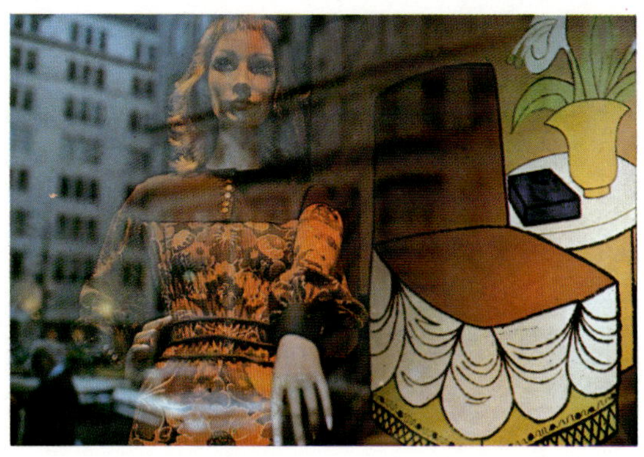

A "straight" shot of a shop window shows the merchandise obscured by reflections and glare.

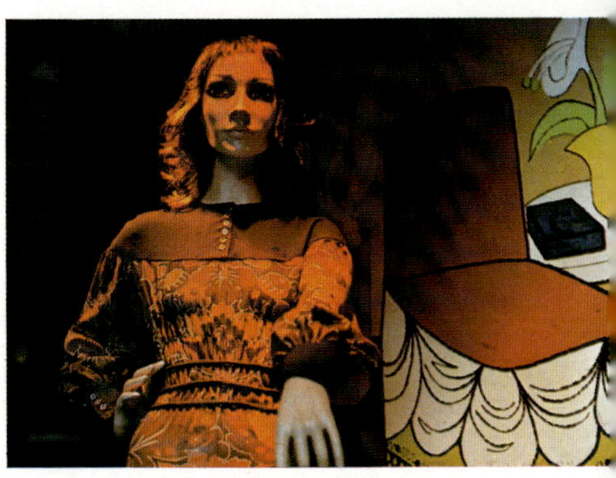

Use of a polarizer eliminates reflections and brings out the underlying colors of the display.

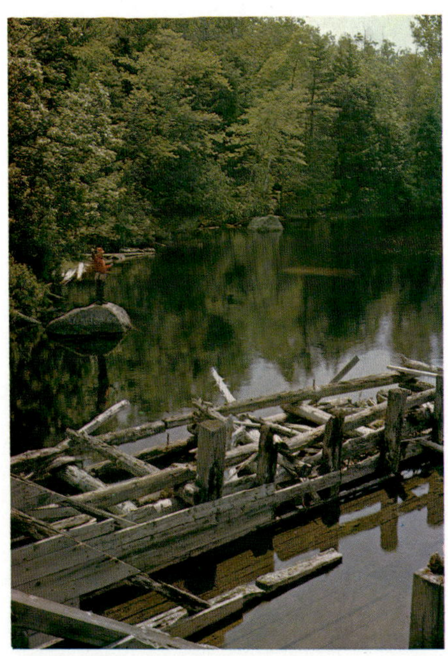

A "straight" shot of a lake in the woods; note sky reflections in water, glare on leaves.

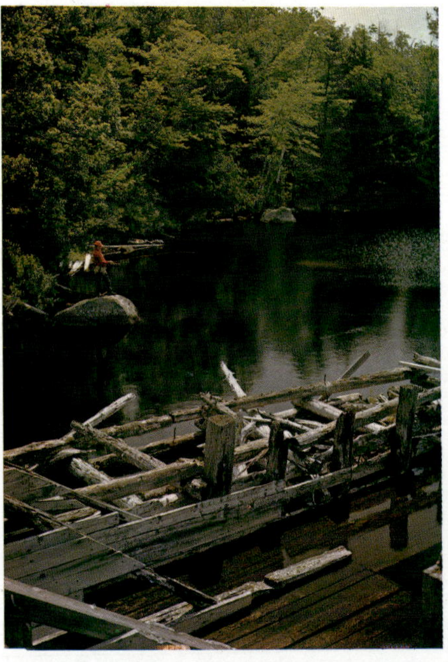

Use of a polarizer eliminates glare on water and leaves and leads to a more colorful picture.

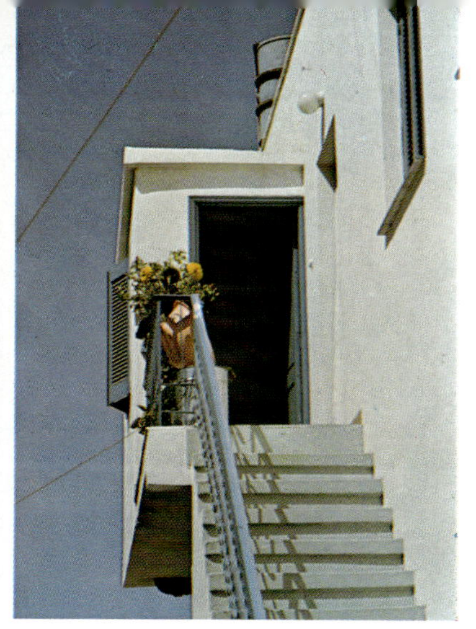

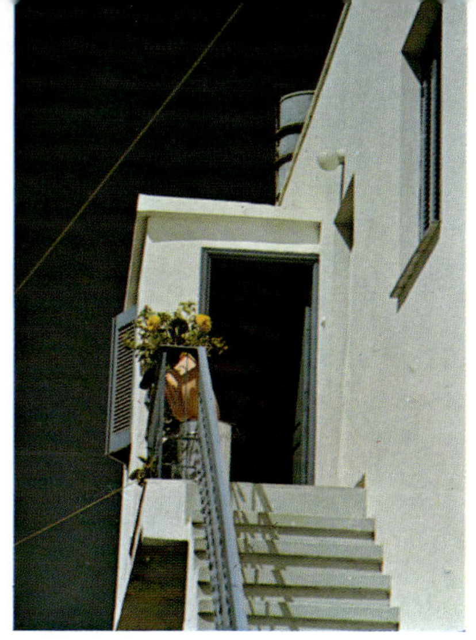

The left one of these two otherwise identical pictures was shot without, and the right one with, a polarizer. Note that in the filtered shot the sky is rendered much darker, although the rendition of all the other colors including white is the same.

Glare and sky control through use of a **POLARIZER**

A polarizer is a filter that mitigates or eliminates reflections and glare on glass, water, polished and varnished wood, shiny paper, glossy paint, and other reflecting surfaces *except metallic ones,* which remain unaffected, thereby enabling a photographer to bring out and intensify the underlying color. In addition, it permits him to darken somewhat a pale blue sky in a region at right angles to an imaginary line connecting the camera and the sun, without affecting the other colors of the scene. Good results can be achieved if the angle of reflection is somewhere between 40° and 70°. At larger or smaller angles, the effect decreases progressively, reaching zero at 90°.

To use a polarizer correctly, hold it in front of your eye and observe the subject while slowly rotating the filter-like disk. At the desired degree of extinction of glare, stop rotating, then slip the disk *in exactly the same position* onto the lens. If you work with a single-lens reflex camera, observe the effect directly on the groundglass while slowly rotating the polarizer previously placed in front of the lens. The exposure factor for most polarizers lies between 2½ and 3, *i.e.*, the diaphragm must be opened up from 1 to 1½ *f*/stops beyond the value indicated by the exposure meter; consult the manufacturer's instructions.

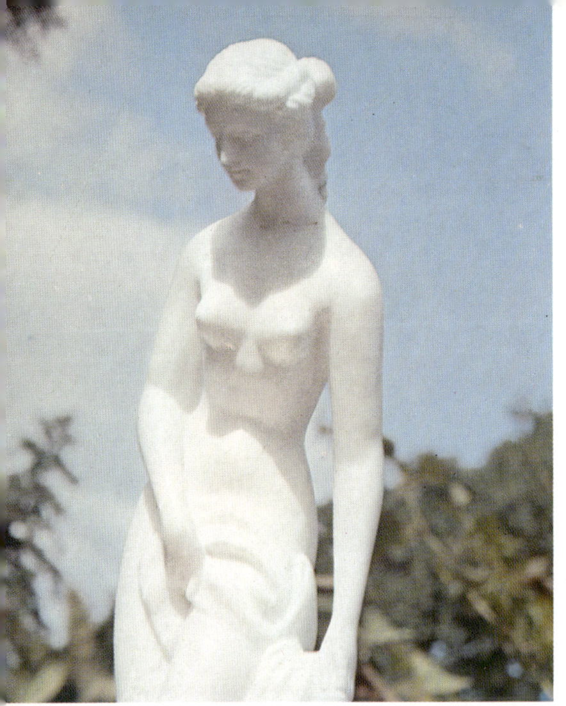

"White," standard daylight.

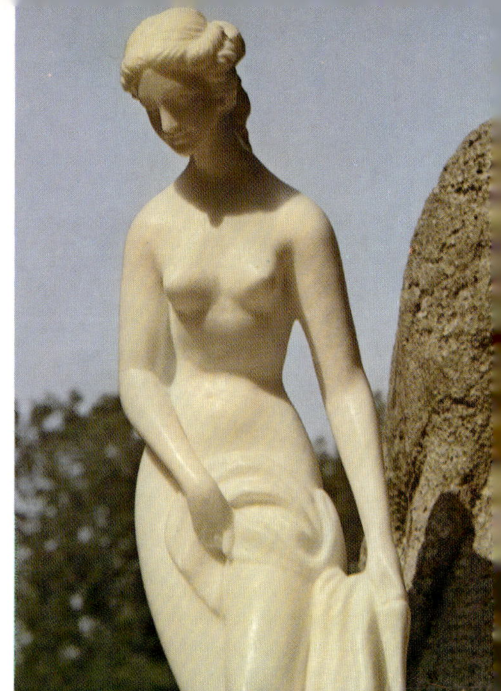

Yellow afternoon light.

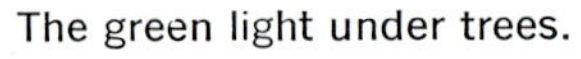

The green light under trees.

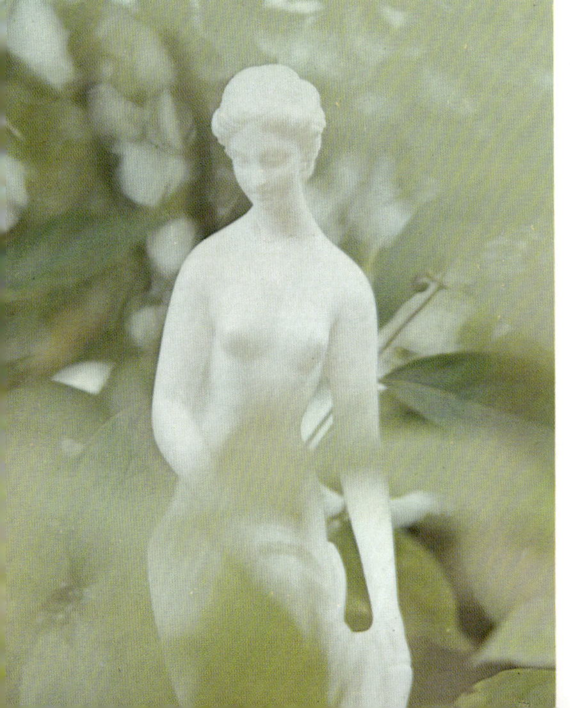

The different colors of DAYLIGHT

Daylight color film is "balanced" for use with *standard daylight*, which is defined as a combination of direct sunlight and light reflected from a clear blue sky with a few white clouds during the hours when the sun is more than 20° above the horizon.

Under different conditions, however, daylight is no longer "white" as far as the color film is concerned, and the overall color of transparencies will therefore deviate more or less toward yellow, red, purple, green, or blue. Should the photographer desire, he can, of course, "correct" the color of non-standard daylight with the aid of filters, as explained on pp. 86–89. More interesting results, how-

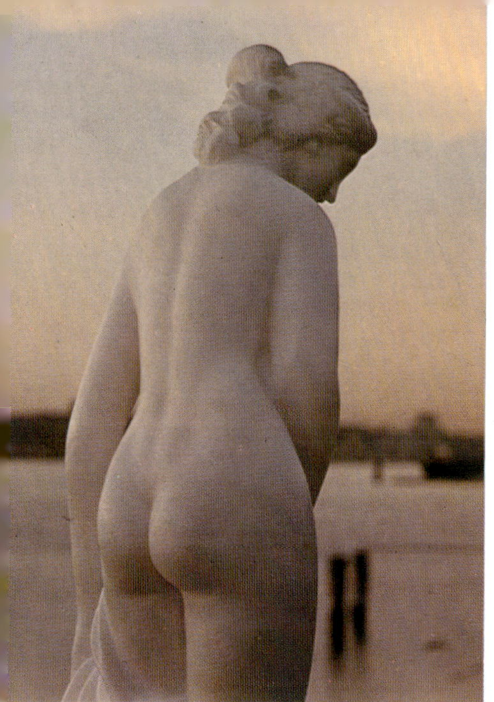

Reddish evening light.

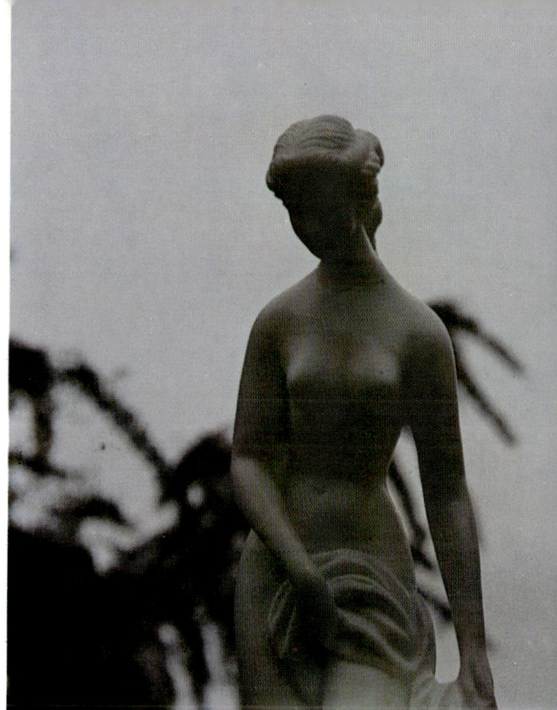

The blue light at dusk.

ever, can often be achieved if the photographer deliberately utilizes such "abnormal" color to produce pictures that literally show the subject "in a new light," different from the ordinary, stereotyped view.

In this connection, the blue overall tone of pictures taken in the open shade, with the subject illuminated exclusively by blue skylight, does not represent "color distortion" but is a perfectly natural and "true" phenomenon: colored light superimposing its own color upon the color of the subject. (See picture at right; note mirror reflecting blue sky—identical in color to the shaded parts of the "white" statuette.) Instead of "correcting" this kind of color, creative photographers use it to make their pictures more interesting and colorful.

Outdoors, shadows are blue.

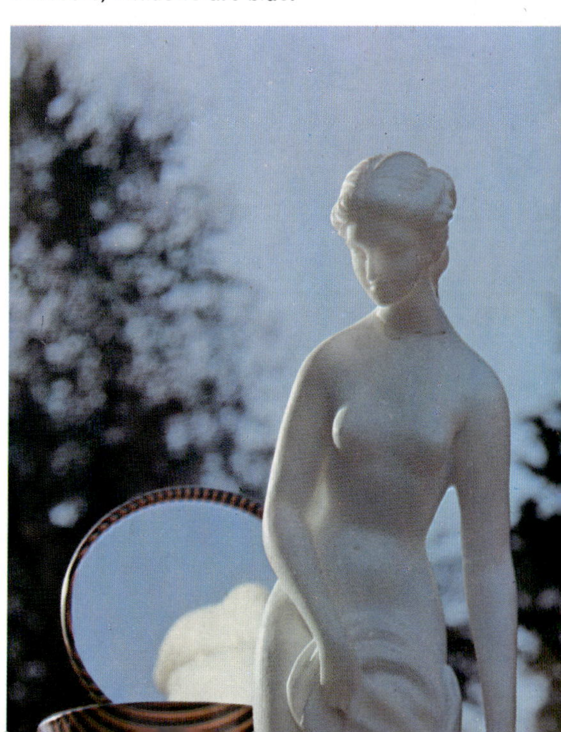

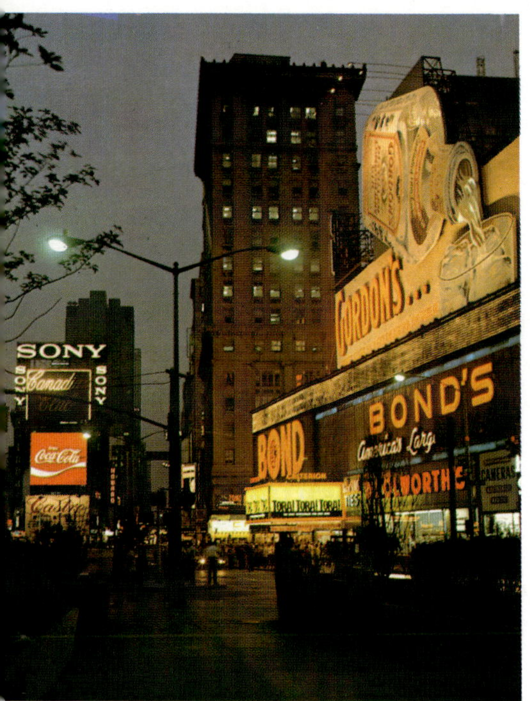

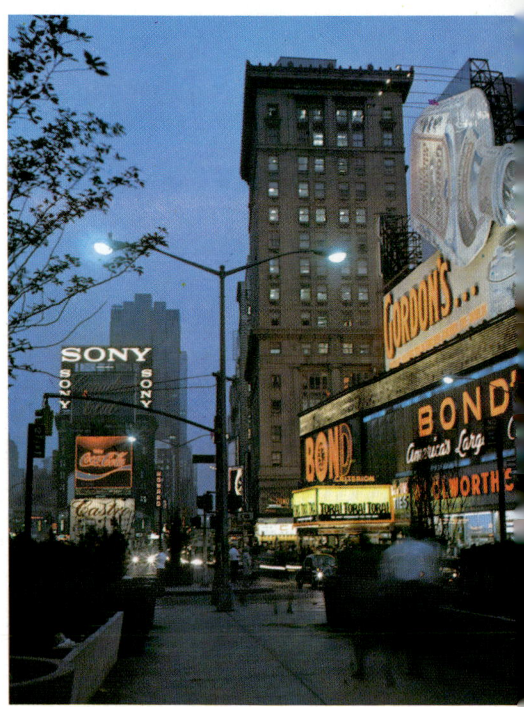

These two photographs were taken within minutes of one another, the left one on daylight color film, the right one on Type B. As always in cases of a mixture of daylight and artificial light, daylight color film produces transparencies with a warmer overall tone than Type A or Type B color film.

Daylight color film, Type A, or Type B?

In cases in which a color photograph must be taken either in a mixture of daylight and artificial light or in fluorescent light, the decision whether to use daylight-type or artificial-light color film depends on the photographer's taste, for neither film will produce completely natural-appearing transparencies, not even with the most refined filtration.

Under such circumstances, the photographer must make up his mind whether he prefers a slightly "warmer" rendition tending toward yellow, in which case he must use a daylight-type color film. Conversely, if he prefers a somewhat "colder" and more bluish rendition, he must use either Type A or Type B color film (p. 24). The accompanying picture pairs show the respective effects.

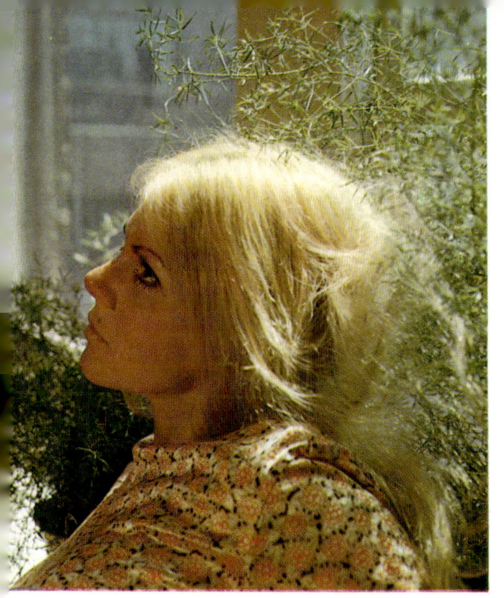

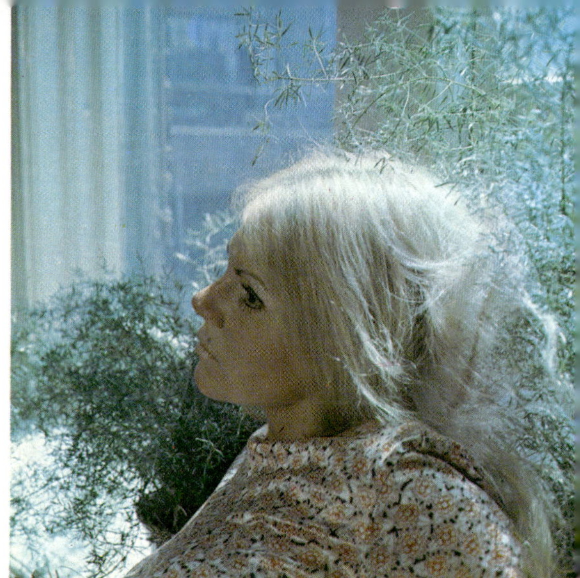

Sunlight streaming through large windows was here combined with photoflood illumination for shadow fill-in. The left photograph was made on daylight color film, the right one on Type B film. Of the two, the left picture, although abnormally "warm" seems to create an impression more in harmony with the subject than the right one, which appears excessively "cold."

Pair of photographs taken in fluorescent light, the left one on daylight color film, the right one on Type B film. Neither one produced "true" color. In this case, filtration in accordance with the film manufacturer's recommendation would probably have improved color rendition somewhat but not to the point where color would be rendered as correctly as if photographed on the proper color film in the proper light.

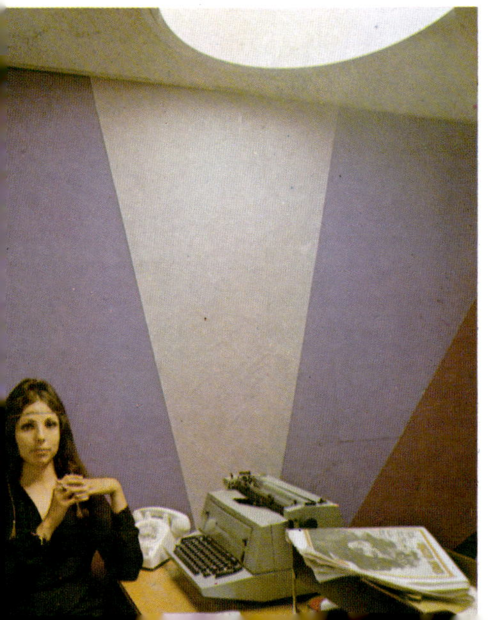

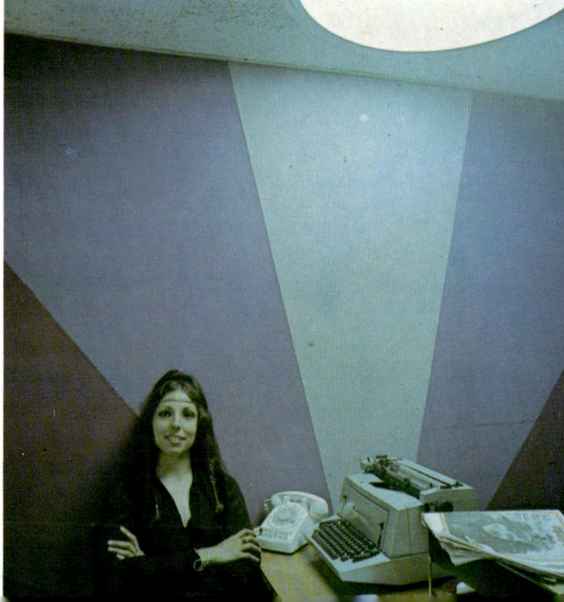

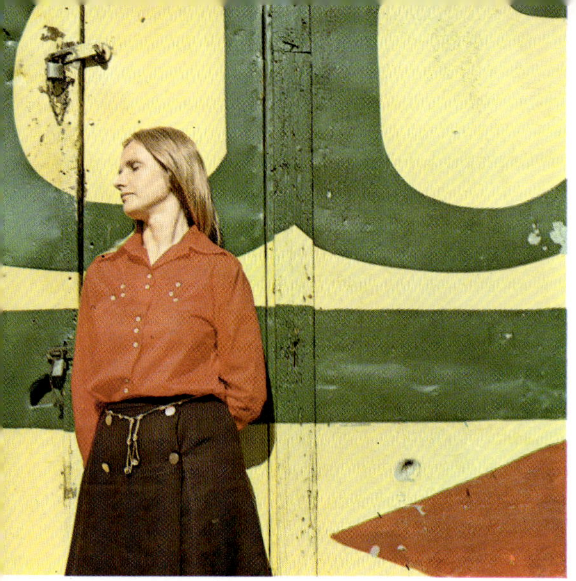

Front light.

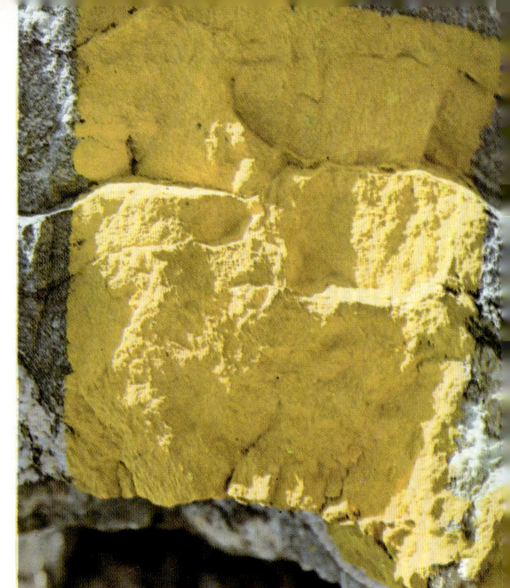

Side light.

The DIRECTION of light

As far as the direction of the incident light is concerned, photographers have the choice of five main types of light, each with its own specific characteristics:

Front light (above, left)—light source behind the camera—is the best type of light for accurate rendition of color. On the other hand, because it throws few or no visible shadows, it easily creates a flat effect and the picture seems to lack depth.

Sidelight (above, right), by throwing shadows visible from the camera position, creates the illusion of space and depth and is excellent for emphasizing texture. However, being the most commonly used type of light, it rarely produces unusual or exciting effects.

Top light (not shown here) is the typical high-noon light—harsh, contrasty, and more or less shadowless. It is the least photogenic type of light, and experienced photographers avoid it.

Light from below (not shown here), which is very rare in nature but easily produced artificially, usually leads to contrived effects, like those produced by footlights.

Backlight (right)—light source behind the subject—because it is the most contrasty type of light and involves the danger of direct light striking the lens and causing flare (pp. 38–39), is the type of light most difficult to use successfully, particularly in color photography.

On the other hand, expertly handled, no other type of light is capable of producing similarly beautiful and striking effects.

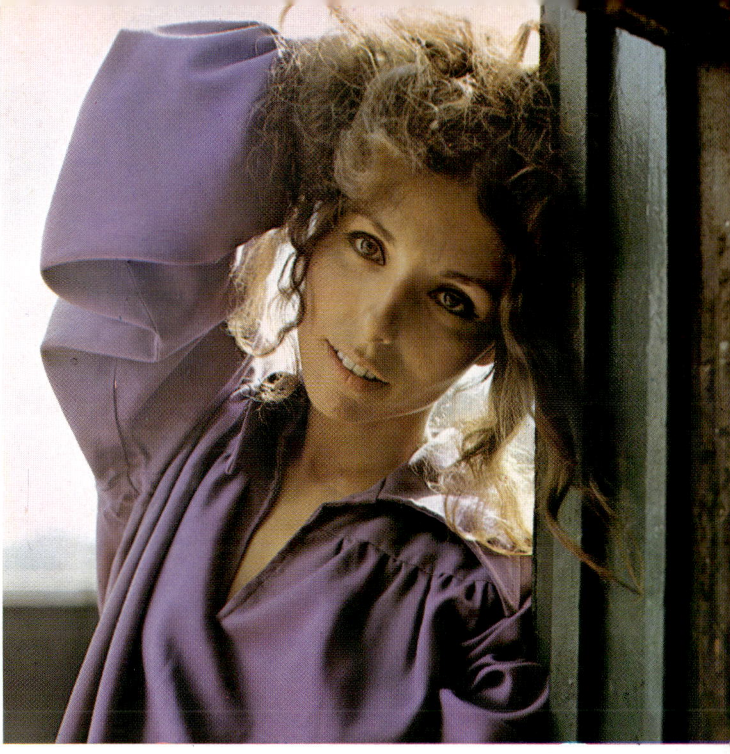

Backlight.

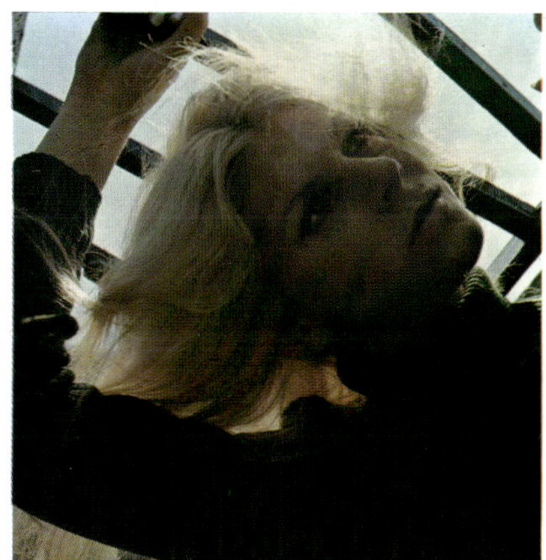

Excessive contrast.

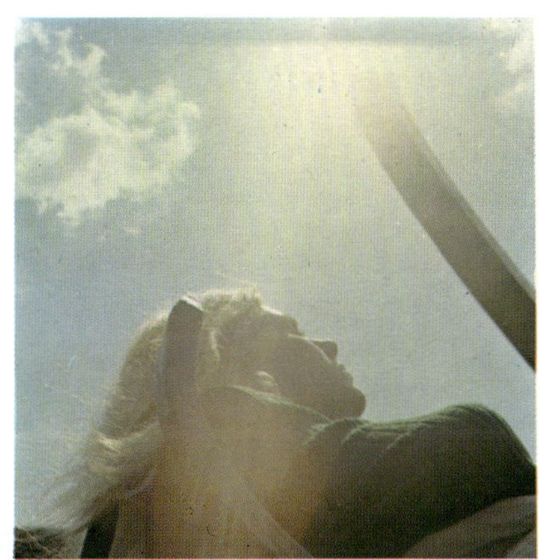

Flare and halation.

The pitfalls of backlight are excessive contrast (left) and flare and halation (right). To avoid, use shadow fill-in illumination (pp. 98–99) for close-ups, make sure direct light does not strike the lens (sun hidden behind a thick branch, a street sign, etc.; photo lamp behind a suitable object or piece of cardboard acting as a shield).

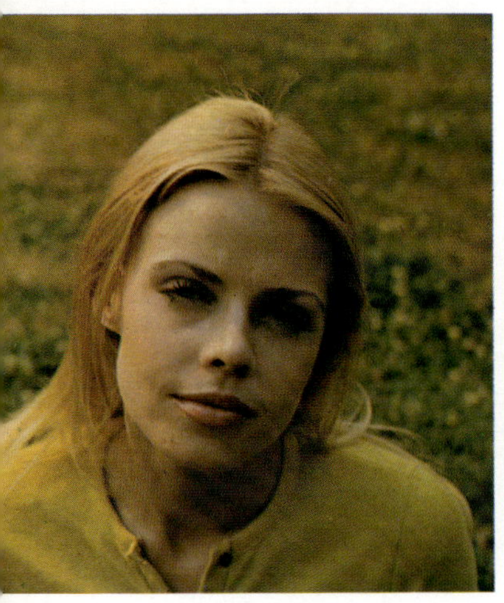

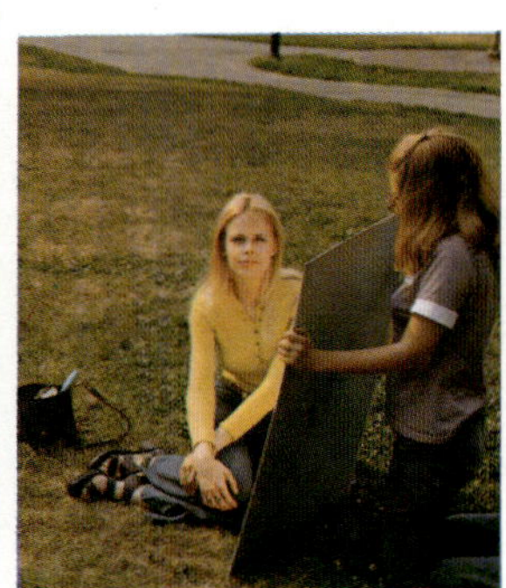

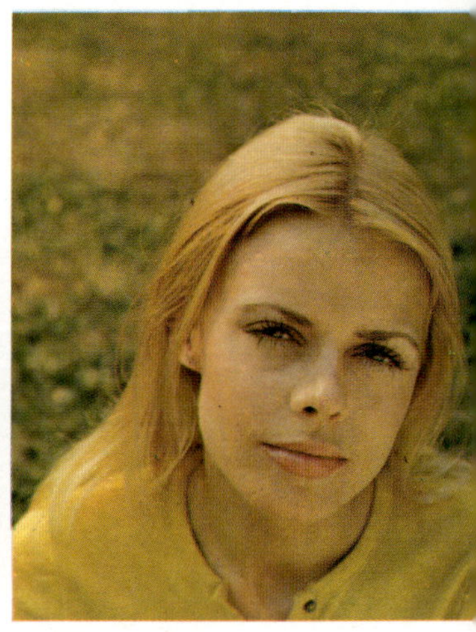

How to balance the illumination in an outdoor close-up. Left: no fill-in illumination used, shadows appear objectionably dark. Center: sunlight reflected upon the shaded part of the face with the aid of a large piece of white cardboard lightens deep shadows. Right: a properly filled in portrait displays low contrast and a pleasant balance between light and shadow.

Better close-ups through SHADOW FILL-IN

Excessive contrast is one of the most common causes of unsatisfactory outdoor-color photographs, particularly of close-ups. Provided that subject distance is not greater than approximately 15 feet, the simplest way to avoid this fault is to reduce undesirably high contrast by means of auxiliary shadow fill-in illumination. This can be done either with the aid of a reflector or with flash.

The simplest reflector is a large sheet of white cardboard held in place by a helper, as shown in the picture above. Somewhat more effective is a sheet of thin plywood covered with finely crinkled aluminum foil. Since the effect is visible, it can easily be controlled.

Flash (pp. 51–53) as a source of shadow fill-in illumination has the advantage that no helper is needed and the disadvantage that it is more difficult to gauge the effect because too much fill-in illumination is as bad as too little. Since some photographers like their pictures more "filled in" than others, the best way to learn how to use this form of contrast control (called daylight flash) is by trial and error on the basis of information furnished by the flash manufacturer. The "sacrifice" of a half dozen test shots is more than made up for by the fact that, once established, such data are valid forever.

Sunlight on a bright day is extremely harsh, making people uncomfortable and causing them to squint.

Therefore, rather than posing his model facing the sun (top, right), an experienced photographer makes outdoor portraits with a combination of backlight and fill-in flash. Prerequisite for success is finding the best ratio between diaphragm stop, shutter speed, and flash intensity; if necessary, the latter can easily be decreased by draping one or several layers of a white handkerchief over the reflector.

A correctly filled-in daylight flash picture is shown at the right, center. When in doubt, too little flash is better than too much (bottom picture), which makes a "flat," overlit, or, in severe cases, "burned out" impression.

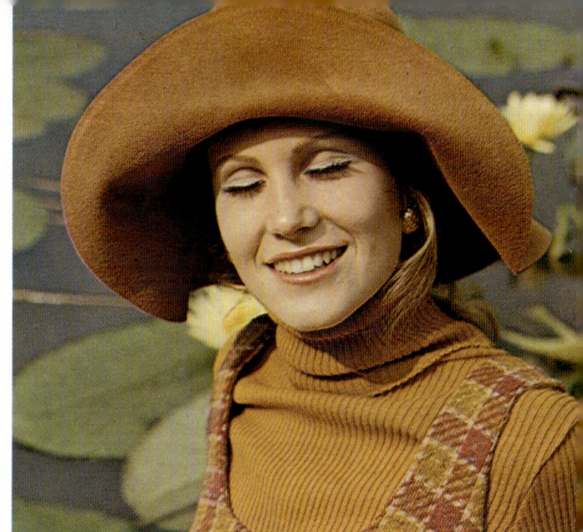

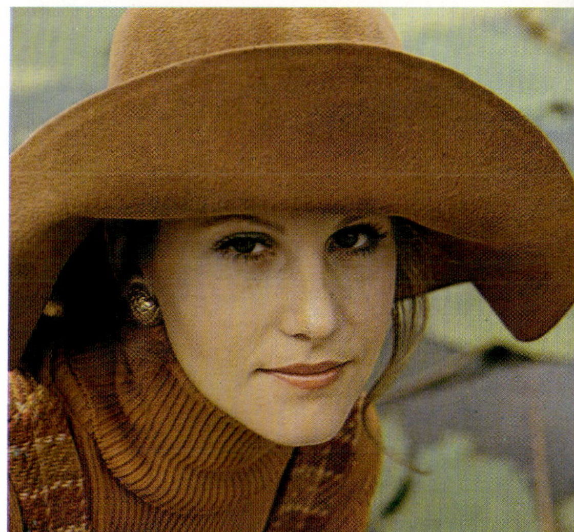

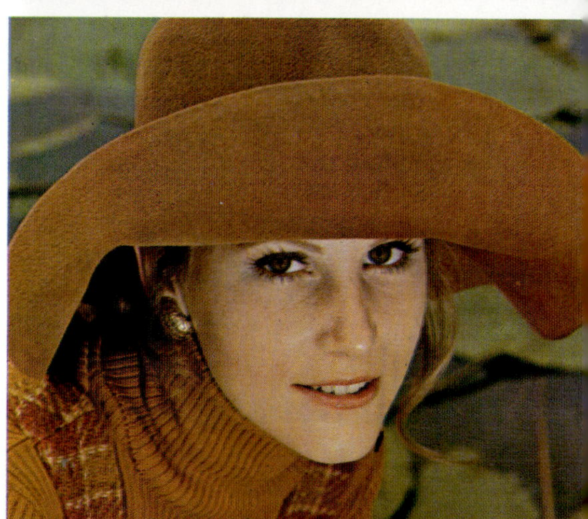

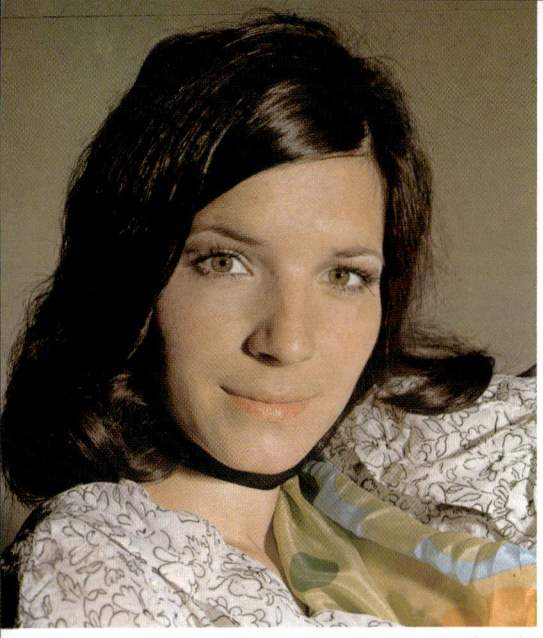

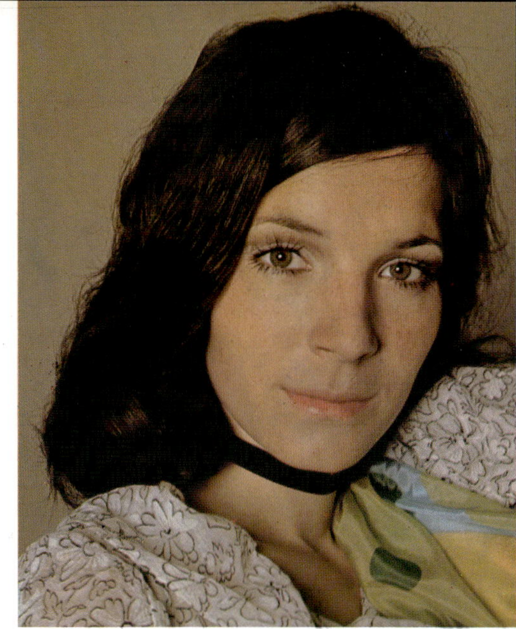

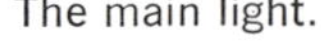

The main light.

The fill-in light.

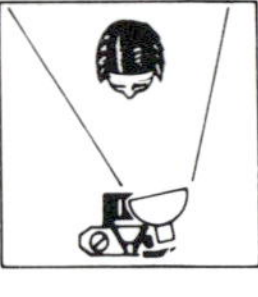

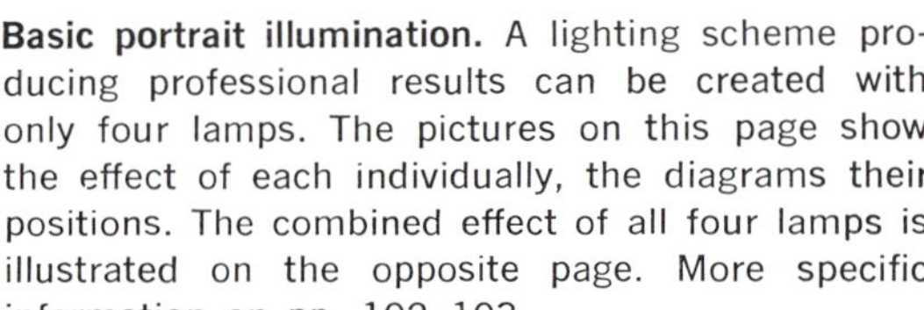

Basic portrait illumination. A lighting scheme producing professional results can be created with only four lamps. The pictures on this page show the effect of each individually, the diagrams their positions. The combined effect of all four lamps is illustrated on the opposite page. More specific information on pp. 102–103.

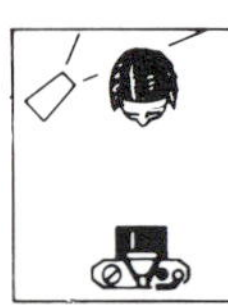

The accent light.

The background light.

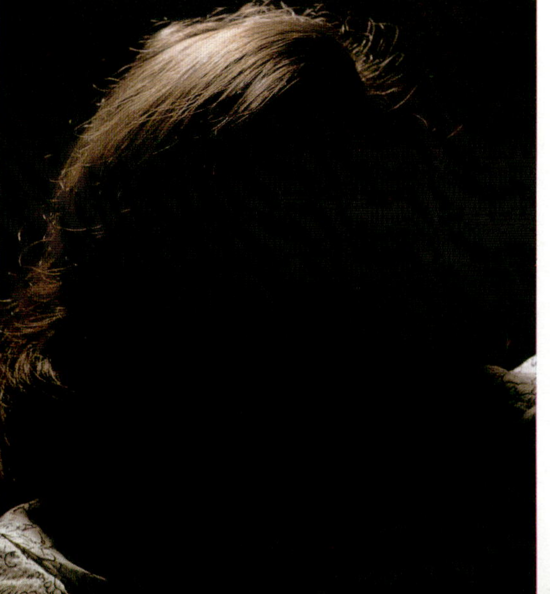

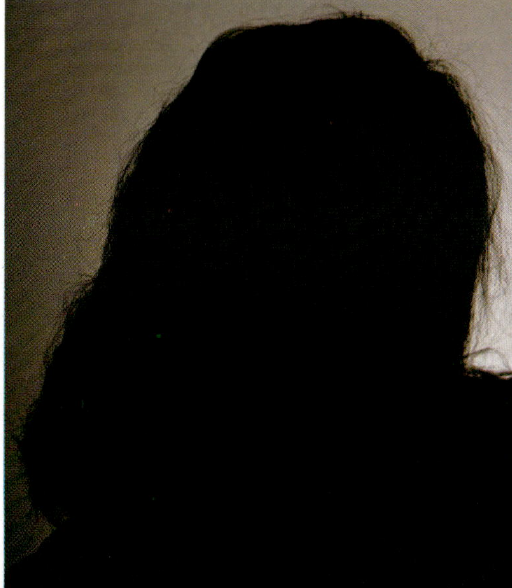

The photograph at the right shows the combined effect of the four lamps, demonstrated individually on the opposite page. The result is "standard illumination"—never very original but never really bad either. Once understood by the photographer, he then can branch out and create more original lighting effects. What can be accomplished in this respect is illustrated by the picture below, which shows the same girl in a more interesting pose and more creative light.

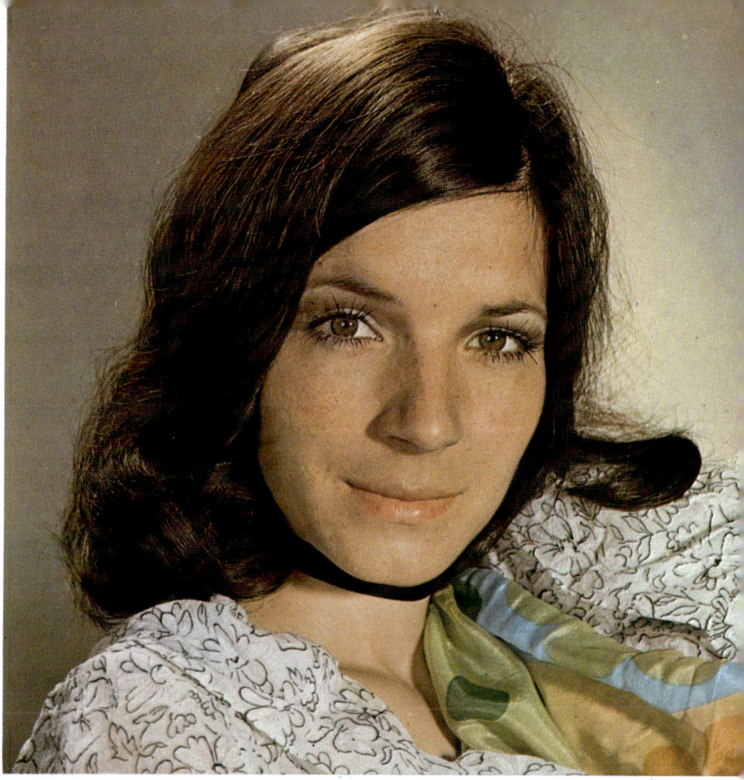

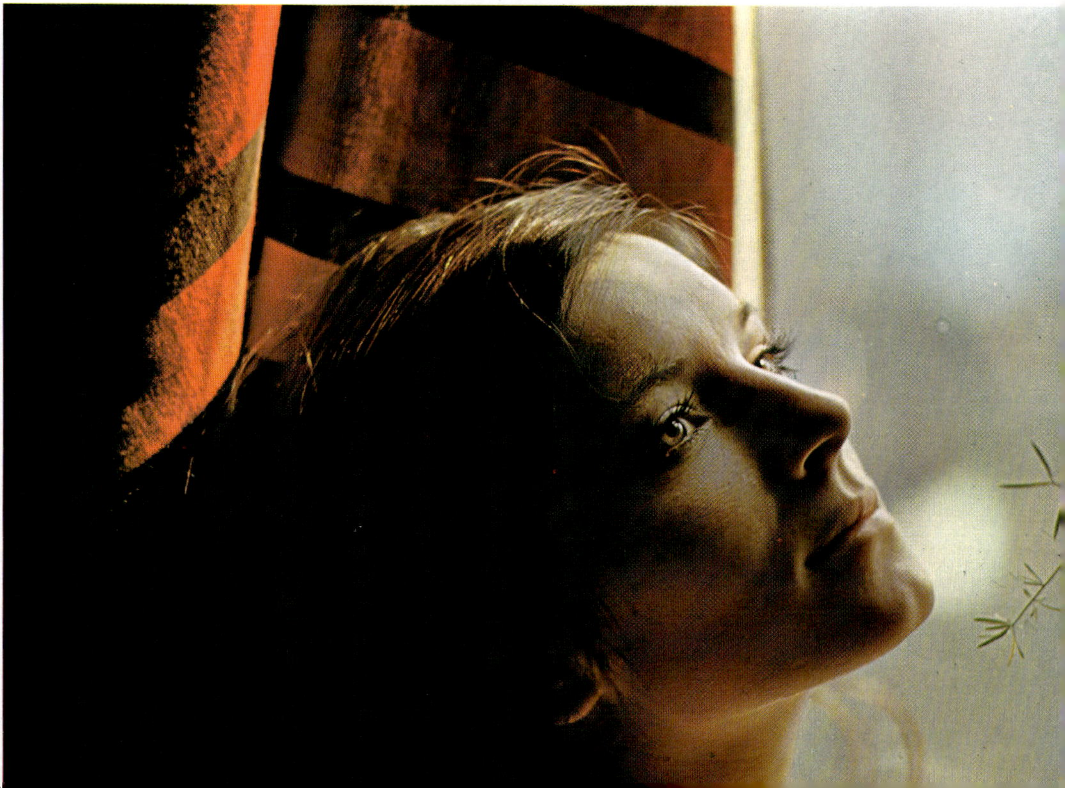

The principles of **GOOD LIGHTING**

The lighting scheme illustrated on the previous spread produces what amounts to "standard illumination." Although never spectacular, it will always lead to satisfactory results, no matter whether the subject is a person or an object, whether the photographer uses incandescent light or flash. It can be modified to almost any extent by varying the angle, distance, and spread of the respective lamps and will still be successful as long as the photographer is familiar with the purpose and effects of the different lights and the following principles that govern any good lighting scheme:

Build your illumination step by step. Never add another lamp until the previous one is placed to your satisfaction.

Always start with *the main light*, preferably a medium-sized spotlight, although a photoflood lamp will do too. It is your most important light. Its purpose is to emphasize the forms of your subject and create a feeling of roundness and depth through proper positioning of the shadows. It also determines the ratio of light to shadow: the more light, the more cheerful, friendly, or feminine the overall effect of the picture; the more shadow, the more severe, somber, and powerful.

Place the *shadow fill-in light* next. Its purpose is to lighten the shadows cast by the main light just enough so that subject contrast does not exceed the contrast range of the color film (pp. 75, 98). A fill-in light should *not* change the character of the main light illumination—too much fill-in light is just as bad as too little—and especially it must not cast secondary shadows, *i.e.*, shadows within the shadows cast by the main light. To avoid this very unsightly fault, use as your fill-in light a photoflood lamp in a *large* reflector equipped with a *diffuser* (p. 54), and place it slightly above but otherwise as *close* to the camera as possible.

Add *the accent light*, preferably a small spotlight. Its purpose is to make the rendition graphically more interesting by adding highlights and sparkle. Since the accent light furnishes backlight (p. 97), care must be taken to prevent it from shining into the lens; a piece of cardboard or another suitable object interposed between the light and the camera outside the field of view of the lens will prevent this.

Place *the background light*, which can be either a photoflood lamp or a spotlight. Its purpose is to separate graphically subject and background by illuminating the background behind the shadow side of the subject while leaving it dark where the subject is light. Without a properly placed background light, the subject can easily appear to "stick to" and even blend with the background.

Whereas most photographers pay considerable attention to the illuminated areas of their subjects, they often neglect the shadows. In this respect, they should consider the following:

In portraiture, the most important shadow is that cast by the nose. It must never cross or even touch the lips.

Other places where ugly shadows might occur are the corners of the eyes near the nose, the angles between the nose and mouth, and beneath the chin. Make sure they receive sufficient fill-in illumination.

Ugly shadows on the background can spoil an otherwise pleasing picture. To avoid this possibility, place your subject well in front of the background and your shadow fill-in lamp sufficiently high so that the shadows it casts will be lower than, and hidden behind, the subject. Trying to "burn out" ugly shadows with the aid of an additional lamp is futile—it would only add another set of shadows to the already existing ones.

In color photography, flash at the camera will produce the effect known as "red-eye" if the model looks directly at the lens: the pupils appear bright red due to light reflected by the retina. To avoid this rather ugly phenomenon, place your fill-in lamp about a foot higher than the camera in cases in which the model looks straight at the lens.

An underlighted background is one of the most common faults in indoor color photography. To avoid it, use an incident-light meter or a Kodak Neutral Test Card in conjunction with a reflected-light meter, and check the illumination levels of subject and background, making sure that both receive the same amount of light. If necessary, rearrange your illumination accordingly.

Single flash at the camera produces the pictorially worst kind of illumination, and too much light or too many lamps can ruin any lighting scheme.

Photography by INCANDESCENT LIGHT

In contrast to daylight the light emitted by lamps specifically designed for photographic purposes (pp. 50–54) is predictable and constant in regard to both brightness and color temperature (p. 86), provided, of course, that incandescent lamps are operated at the specified voltage. As a result, correctly exposed color photographs taken in the kind of artificial light for which the color film is designed usually have excellent color. To utilize this potential, however, a photographer must know the following:

Incandescent photo lamps require relatively large amounts of power. To avoid blowing a fuse, calculate the number of photo lamps that can be used simultaneously as follows: multiply the number of amperes of the fuse by the voltage of the power line; the resulting figure represents the number of watts that you can draw safely. For example, if the line carries 120 volts and the fuse (or circuit breaker) is designed for 15 amperes (this is the most common combination), the permissible number of watts is $120 \times 15 = 1800$. This means that you can simultaneously use three lamps of 500 watts each and still have 300 watts left over for ceiling lights and a radio. Alternatively, you could also use two lamps of 500 watts each plus three lamps of 250 watts each and still have a safety factor of 50 watts, and so on.

If more lamps are needed, to avoid blowing a fuse, additional lights must be connected to a different circuit. The simplest way to sort out the different circuits is to plug ordinary lamps into the various outlets and unscrew the fuses one at a time. All the lamps that go out when a certain fuse is disconnected belong to the same circuit, whereas the lamps that stay lit are controlled by a different fuse.

The fuse, the safety valve of the power line, is designed to give under an overload in order to save the line itself from destruction. Therefore, an accidentally blown fuse must never be replaced by a stronger one, or a coin, or a wad of aluminum foil. Otherwise, the next overload would melt the power line and the resulting short circuit could start a fire, which might burn down the house.

The chances of accidentally blowing a fuse can be virtually eliminated by taking the following precautions:

Buy only electrical equipment or wiring that carries the UL (Underwriters Laboratory) label. It is a guarantee that they meet certain minimum safety standards, which merchandise lacking this label may not meet.

Inspect your wires periodically and replace all those with cracked, frayed, gummed, or otherwise damaged insulation or defective plugs.

Do not overload your wires. Touch the wires after the lamps have been burned for some time; they may get warm but should never be allowed to get uncomfortably hot. If they do, the copper strand inside the cord is too thin to carry the load, and a short circuit might be incipient. In such cases, a heavier gauge wire must be used.

When disconnecting an electric wire, do not hold onto the cord and jerk; instead, grip the plug and pull it out straight.

Place temporarily strung wires so that people cannot trip over them. Lead them along the walls or furniture, or cover them with a rug.

Rubber-insulated electric wires should never be nailed or stapled to baseboards, walls, or ceilings. Depending on the local building code, only metal-sheathed cables or flex can be used for permanent installations, and only a licensed electrician should install them.

Do not reconnect electrical equipment that caused a fuse to blow without first finding and eliminating the cause of the short circuit.

Do not indiscriminately fire flashbulbs with house current (for example, by screwing them into a table lamp to simulate its original lighting effect). Although they may fit the lamp socket, they might also blow a fuse. However, you may safely fire with house current of up to 125 volts the General Electric Nos. 22 and 50 and Sylvania Nos. 2 and 3 flashbulbs. If you wish to fire two or more flashbulbs simultaneously, connect a large incandescent bulb in series to absorb the shock and avoid blowing the fuse.

A CREATIVE APPROACH TO COLOR

Color is a very personal experience that affects different people differently. Some are sensitive to all its subtle tones and shadings, whereas others react only to bold and saturated hues. Furthermore, all body colors and pigments change in appearance with changes in the color of the illuminating light, as a result of which any objects including, of course, people and faces, assume different color shades depending on whether we see them in "white" daylight, yellow early morning light, reddish sunset light, the greenish light of the forest, or the blue light at dusk (pp. 92–93). And finally, photographs of the same subject taken under identical conditions on different brands of color film may be markedly different in regard to color. All of which goes to show that "true" color is a myth and "natural" color rendition an illusion.

The conclusion seems obvious to me: striving for the ultimate in "naturalness" is only one way to good color photography and not necessarily the best one, either. More interesting results are often achieved by photographers who realize the illusive nature of "true" color and search instead for color that is significant, expressive, and beautiful. As a result, open-minded, imaginative photographers have the choice of three ways to good color photography:

Pictures in which *color appears true*, although it may actually be "falsified." This approach may necessitate filtration (pp. 86–89), which, strictly speaking, is "falsification," in order to convert light of the "wrong" color (pp. 92–93) to the type of light for which the color film is balanced.

Pictures in which *color is true*, although it may appear unusual and even "unnatural" because the light that illuminated the subject was not "white" but colored (pp. 92–93), as in shots taken very early or very late in the day, in the bluish light of open shade, or in the green of the forest.

Pictures in which *color is obviously not "true"*, *i.e.*, in which the subject appears very different from the way we are used to seeing it in "white" light (pp. 116–119, 125). This is the field of "experimental" color photography, involving filters in front of the lens and colored gelatins in front of photo lamps, infrared color film (pp. 118–119), color solarization, color posterization (pp. 126–127), and other creative means. Its possibilities are unlimited.

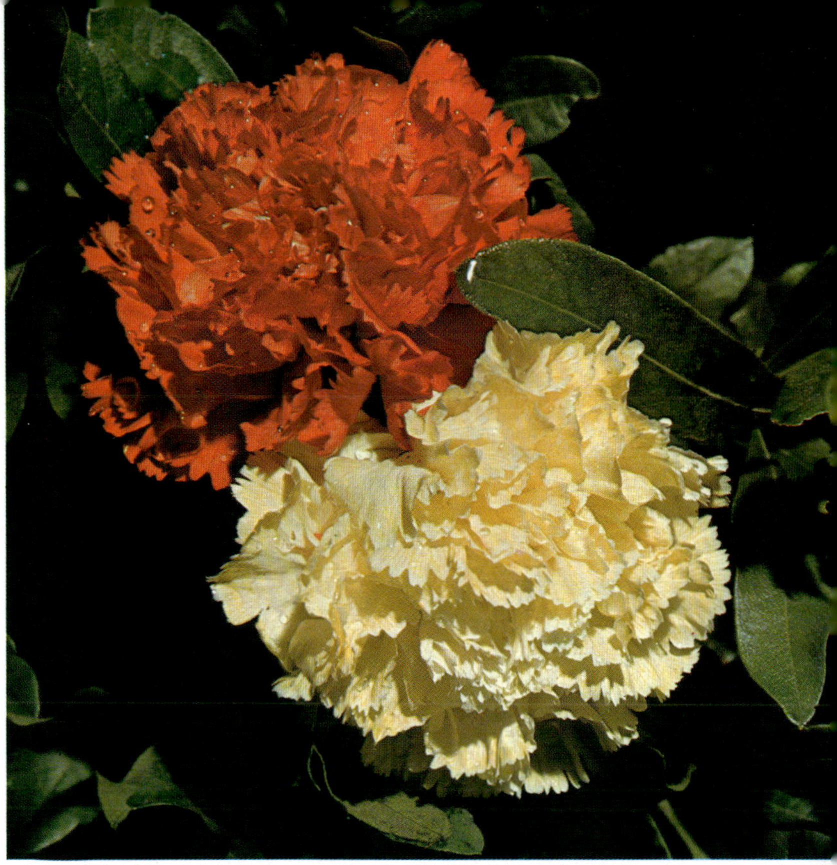

The effective use of color

A common fault made by many color photographers is to try to get too many different colors into the same picture. The overall shot of a garden (right), for example, contains many more different colors than the close-up of a few flowers (above), but the latter, because of its bolder, more concentrated treatment of color, is usually more effective. The lesson is obvious: a few colors, carefully chosen and boldly displayed (pp. 108–115), make a stronger impression than all the colors of the rainbow—in driblets.

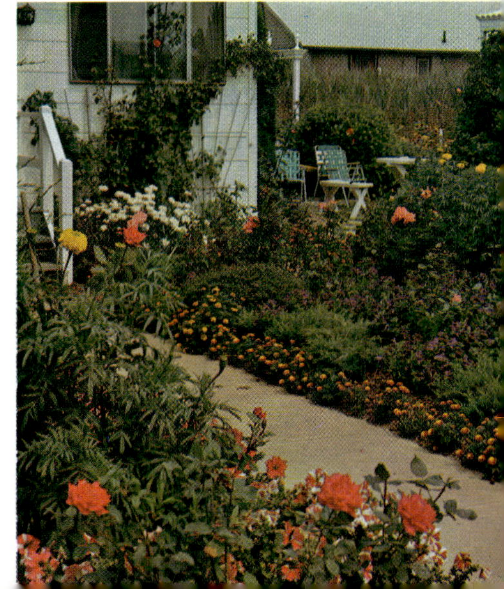

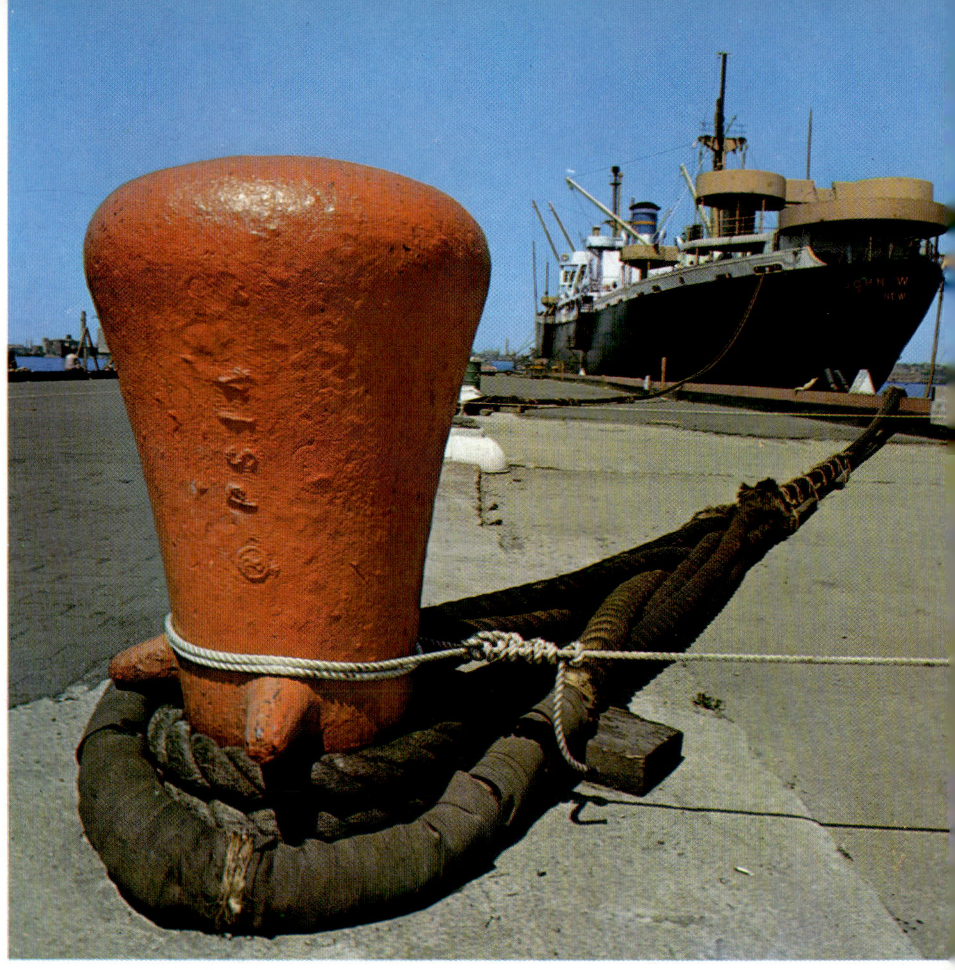

Contrasting and complementary colors

The strongest color effects are always achieved by juxtaposition of two fully saturated, contrasting, or, better still, complementary colors. Physicists call any two colors complementary which, superimposed in the form of colored light, complement one another to form white. More popularly, complementary color pairs are, among others,

red and green,
yellow and blue,
purple and chartreuse.

Photographers who, for one reason or another, wish to give their color shots a strong "poster effect" would do well to utilize the inherent potential of contrasting or complementary color pairs as illustrated by the pictures on this spread.

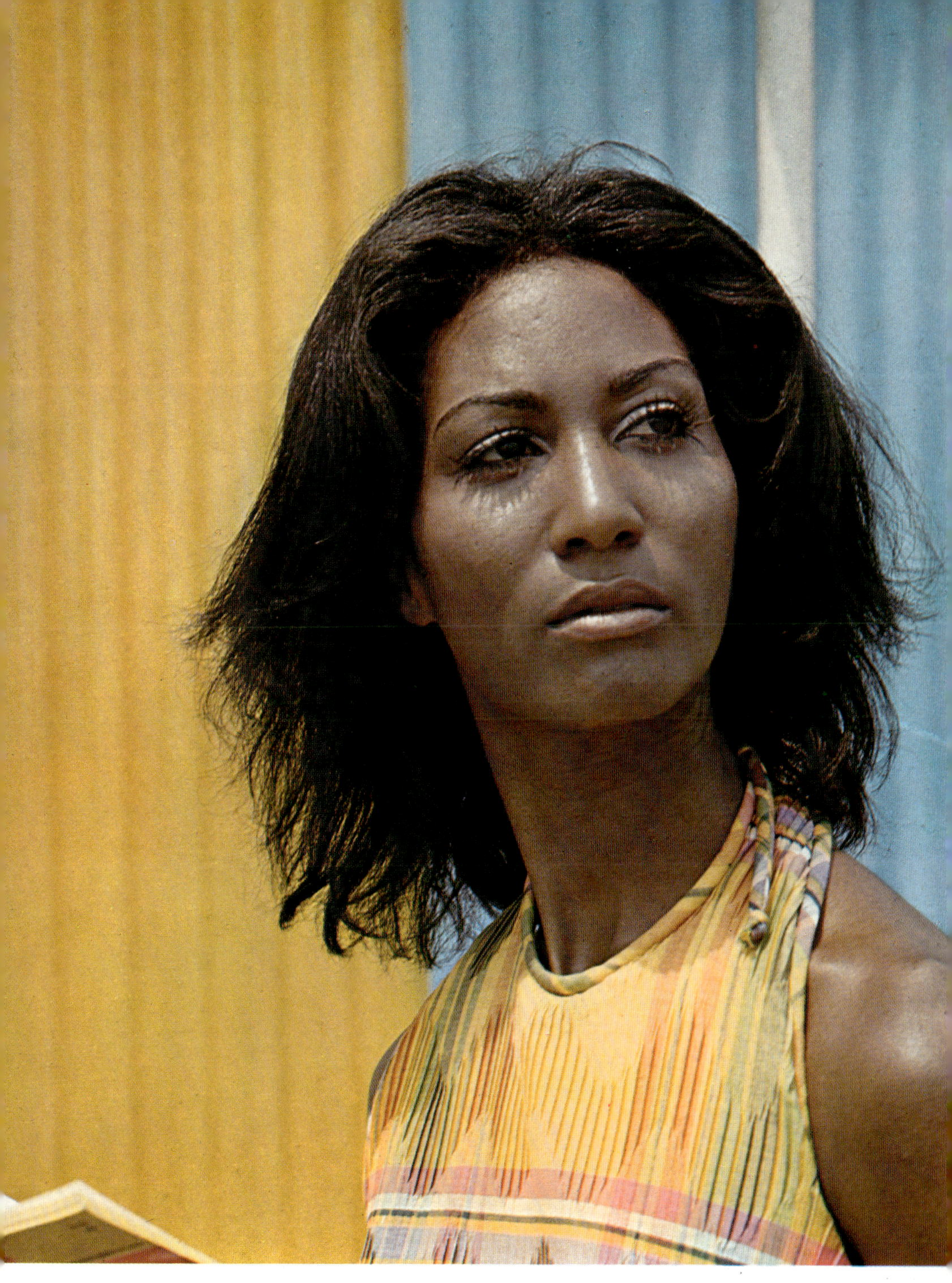

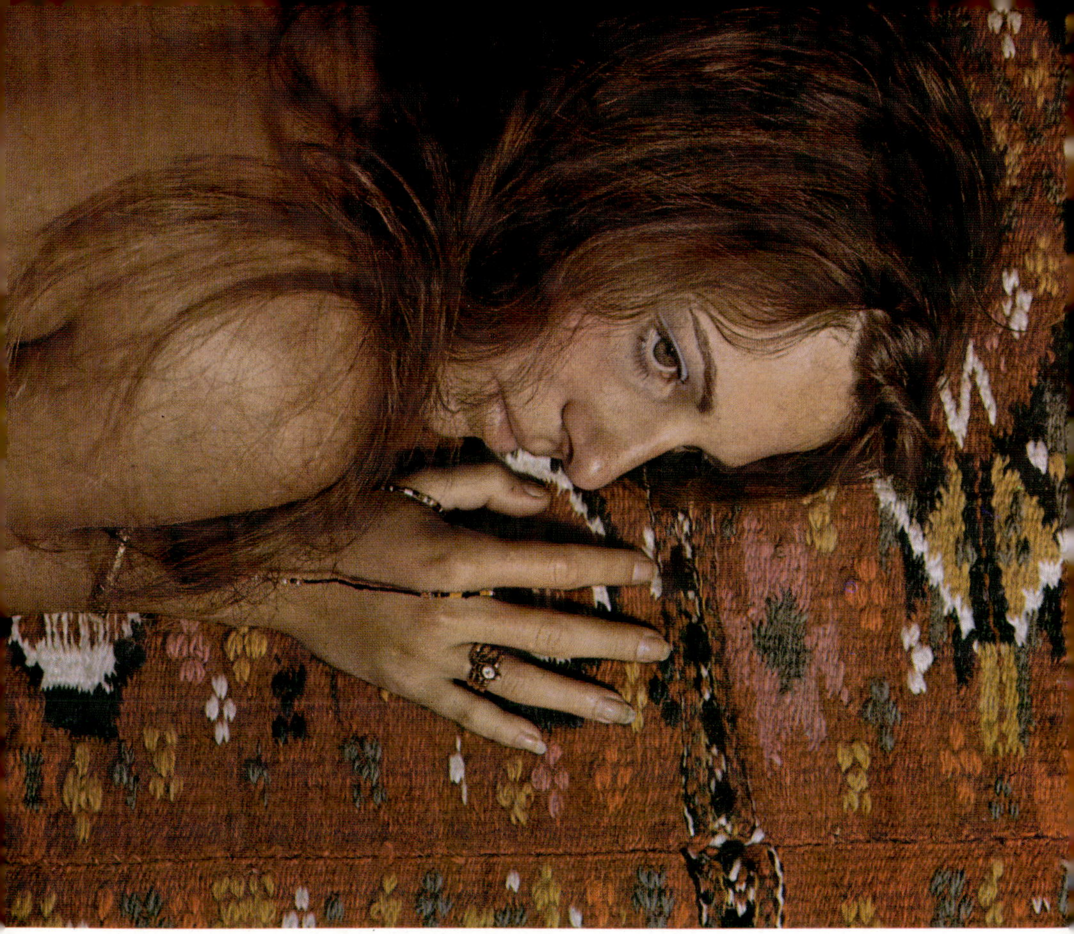

Example of a composition in related colors.

Related and harmonious colors

Colors that, although distinctly different, have certain characteristics in common are related like, for example, the "warm" colors—yellow, orange, red, and brown—or the "cool" colors—blue-green, blue, and purple-blue (which share the common denominator blue). Such colors are neighbors in the Munsell Color Wheel and, in combination, automatically give a color photograph a feeling of unity that is lacking in aggregates of unrelated colors.

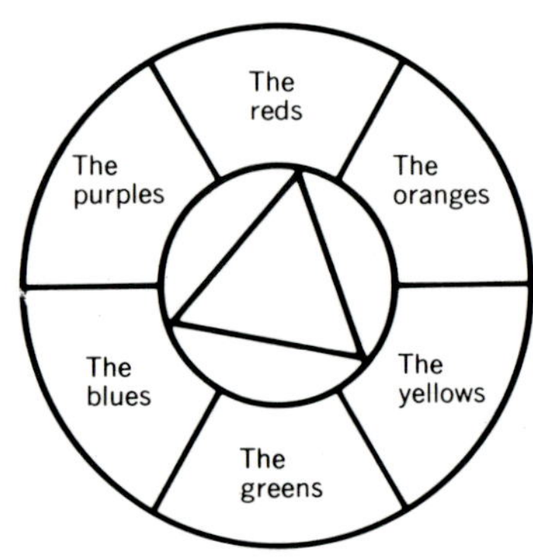

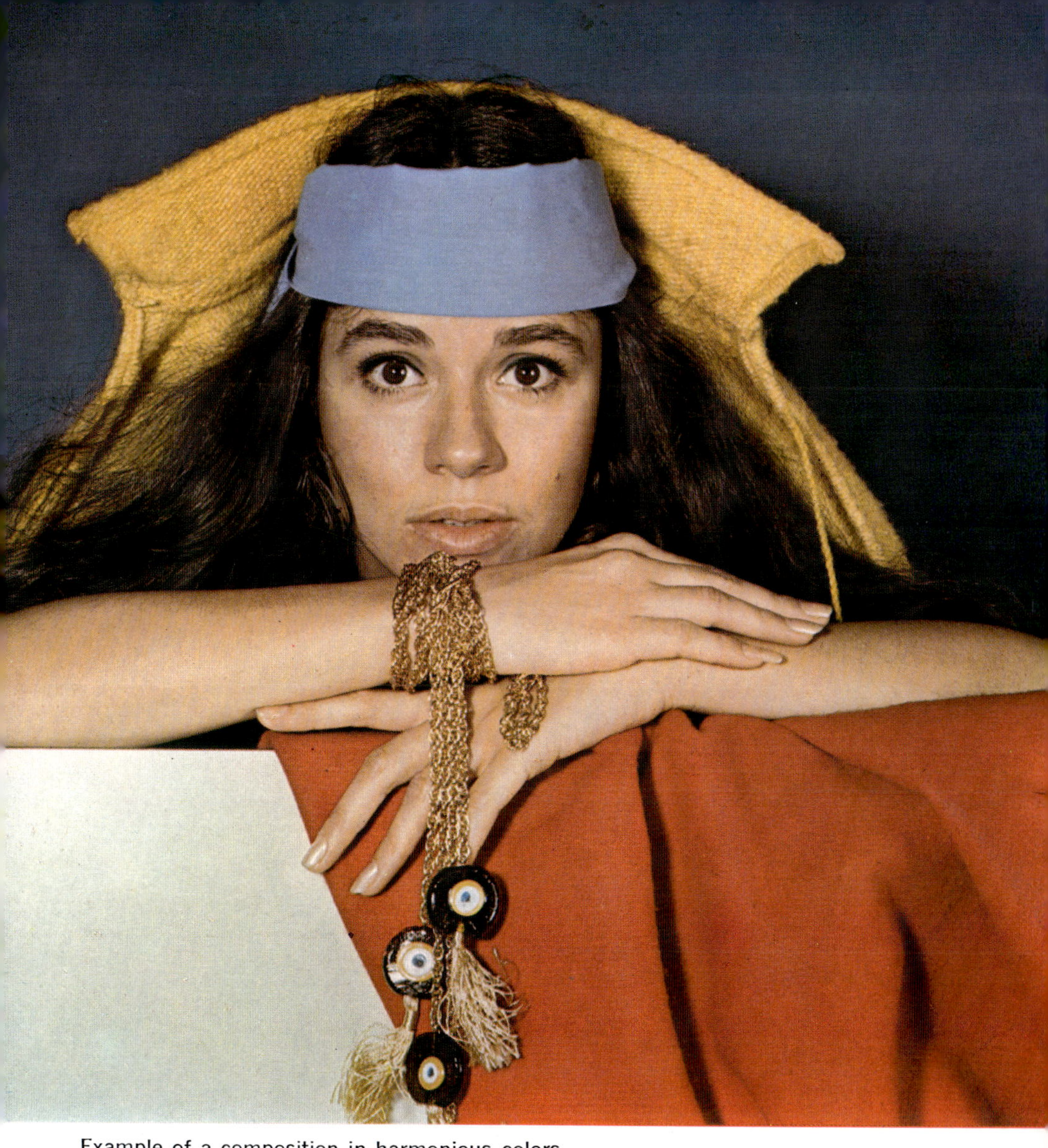

Example of a composition in harmonious colors.

Any three colors connected within the circle of the Munsell Color Wheel by an equilateral triangle are called harmonious, which means that they go well together, like the separate tones that form a chord in music. This axiom is illustrated by the photograph above, which combines the three primaries red, yellow, and blue, emphasized and made still more luminous by the addition of black and white. See explanation on pp. 112–113. Adding non-harmonious colors like, for example, orange or green to a color "chord" consisting of red, yellow, and blue would add a very sour note indeed.

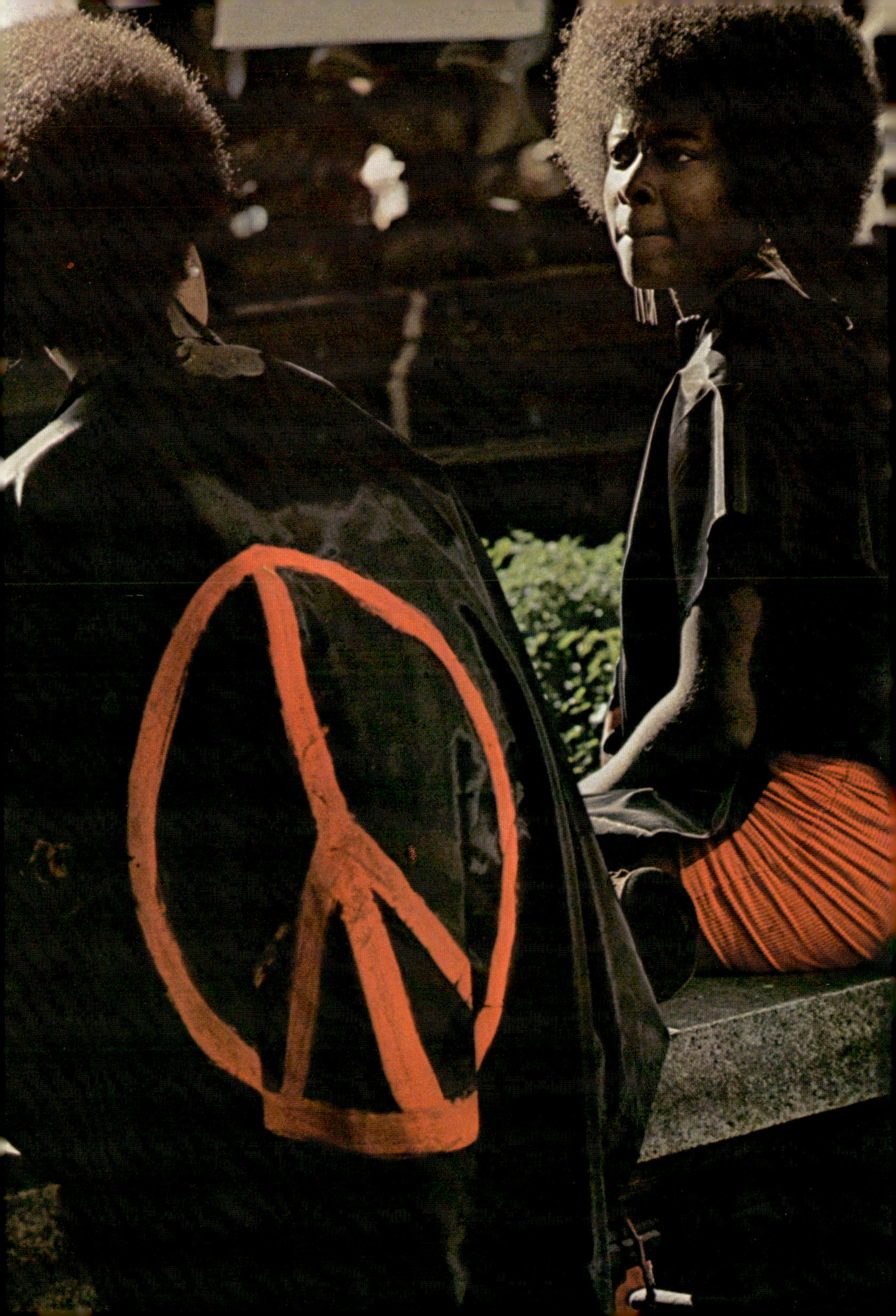

Black, white, and gray as color

Unlike beginners, who think of color in terms of quantity, experienced photographers see color in terms of quality; and they know that black, gray, and white are "colors" that in color photography play the following important roles:

Black and *white* enable a photographer to give his pictures a high-contrast effect without having to pay the penalty in the form of overexposed light colors and underexposed dark colors (since it obviously is impossible to overexpose white or underexpose black). In addition, *black*, by virtue of its depth, makes color—and white!—appear more luminous, whereas *white*, in contrast to its own lightness, makes color—and black!—appear more saturated and deeper. *Gray*, in contrast to its own neutrality, makes color appear more colorful.

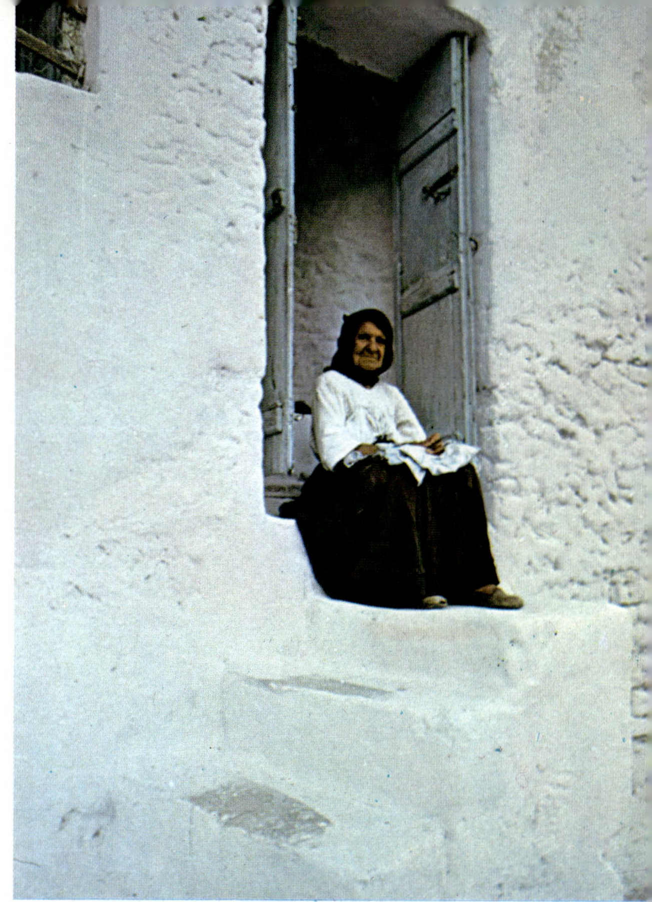

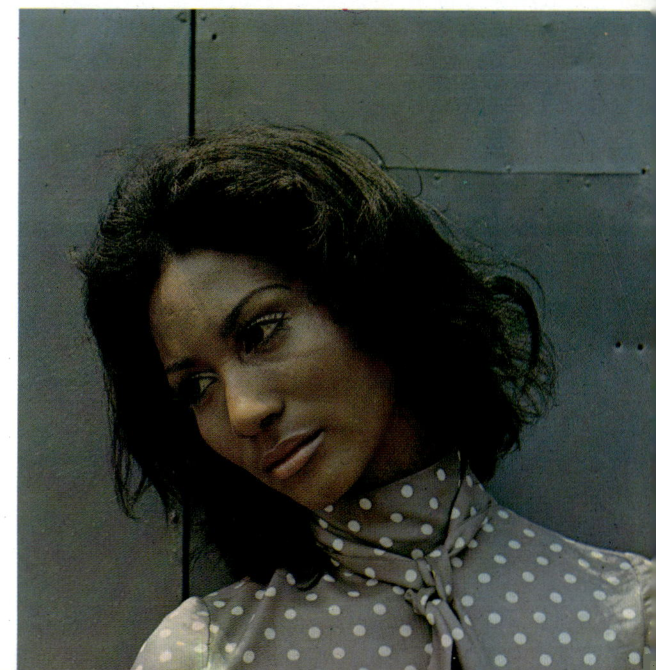

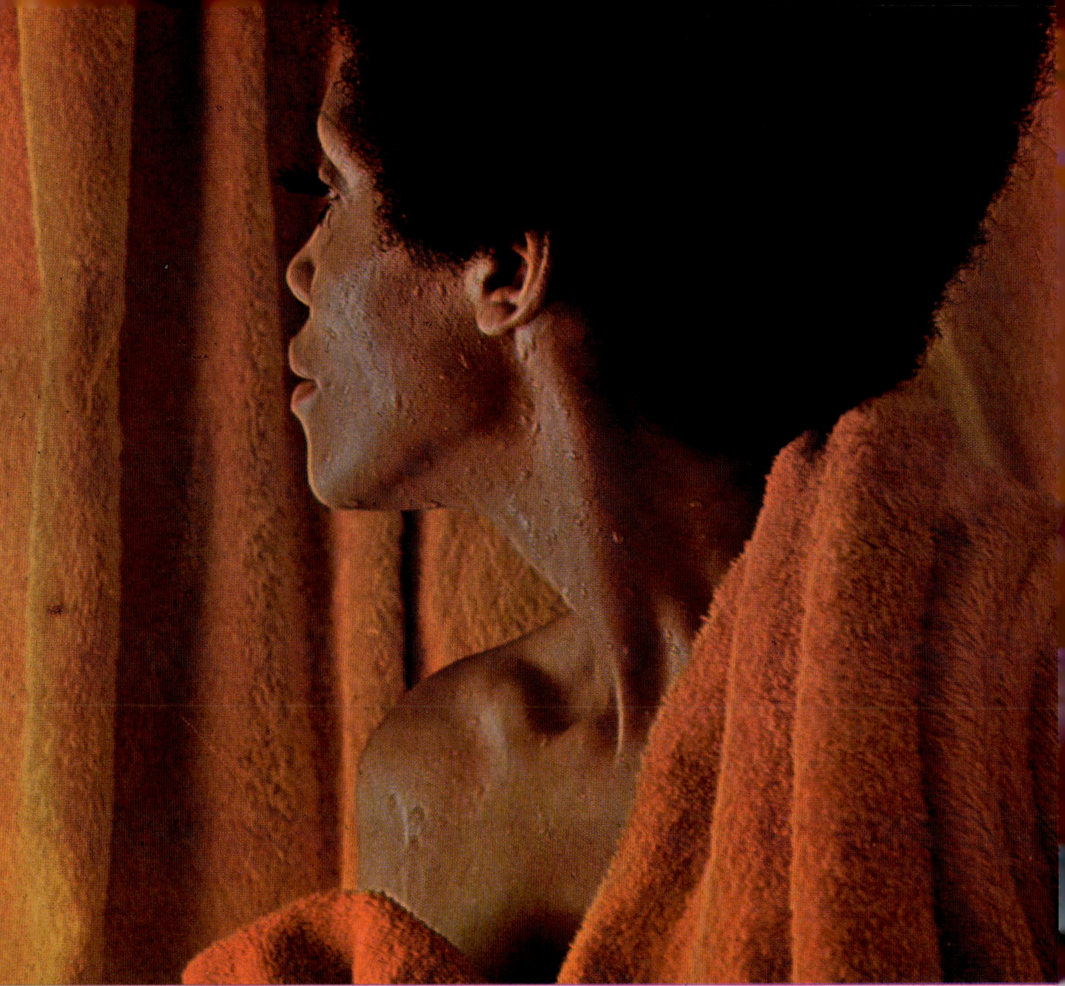

Color monochromes

Many photographers believe that subjects that lack strong, diversified colors are more effective in black and white because they would appear too monotonous if shot in color. Although, at first glance, shooting more or less monochromatic subjects in color may seem a waste of color film, the opposite is frequently true: many such subjects would be less effective in picture form if they were rendered in black and white instead of color, as proved by the photographs shown on this spread. Other examples are scenes taken at dusk when everything is steeped in beautiful, luminous blue; verdure, foliage, green meadows and grass; the soothing gray of rainy days and landscapes shrouded in pearly fog; the snowy white of winter. Depicted in black and white, these and many other "monochromatic" subjects would be the poorer for lack of subtle color shades, ineffective and weak.

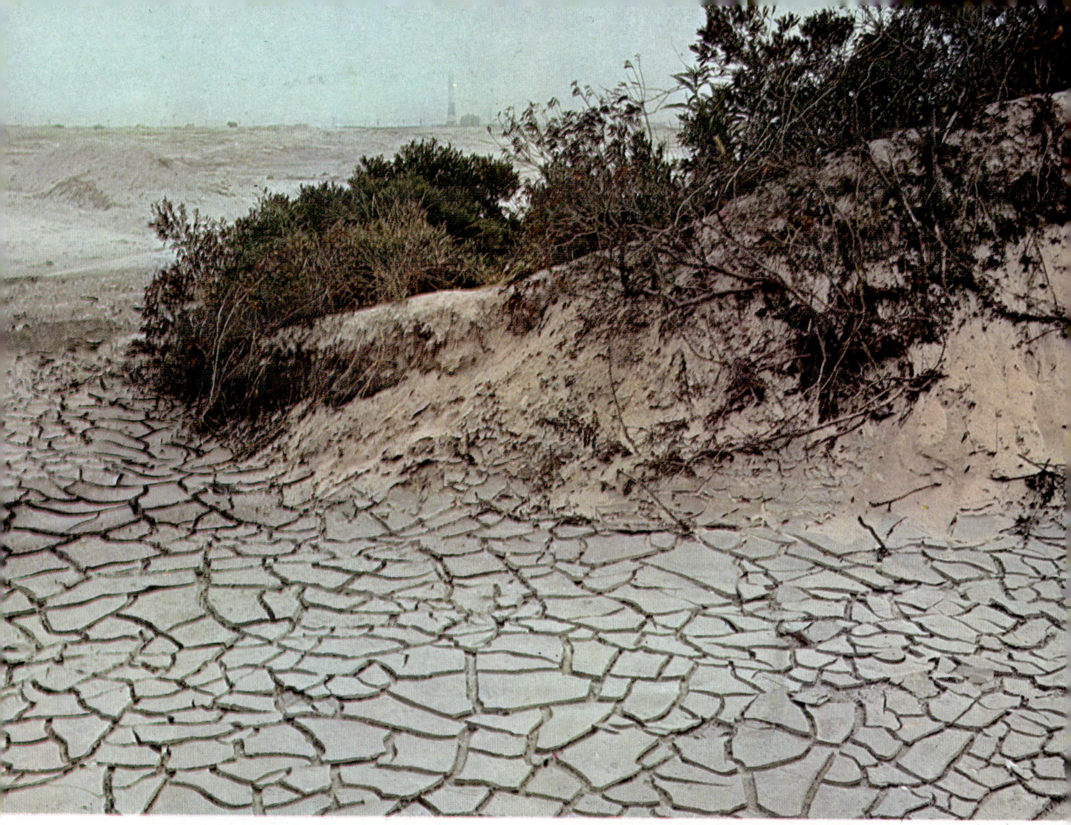

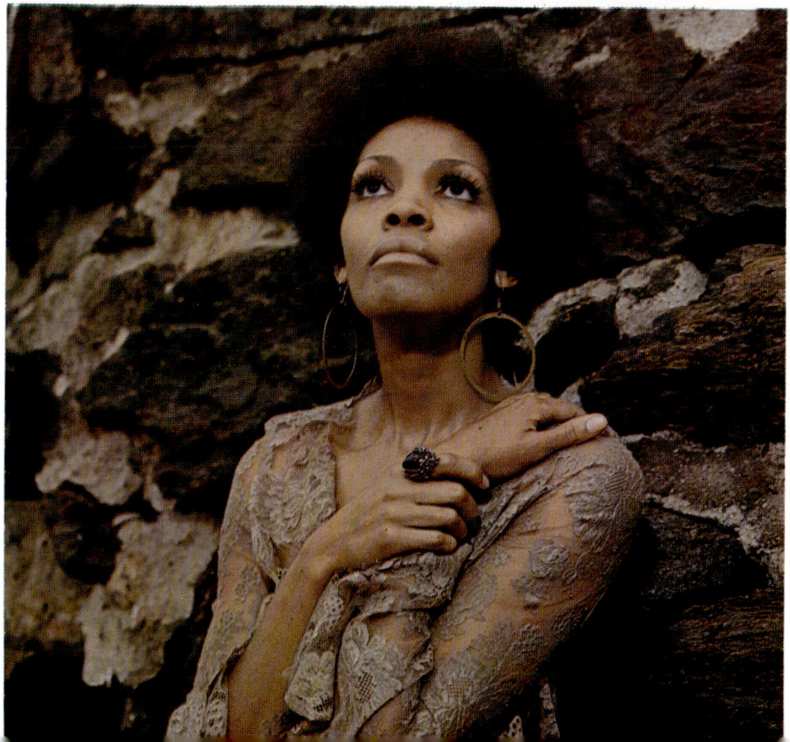

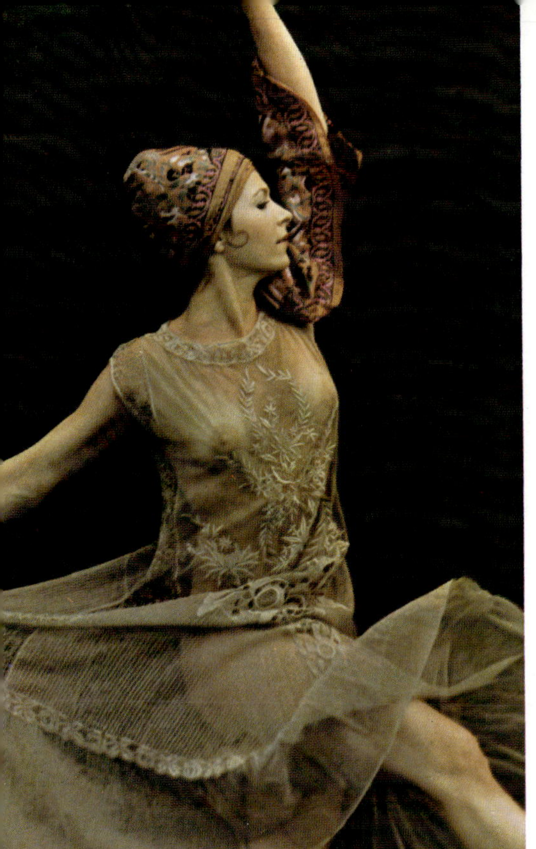

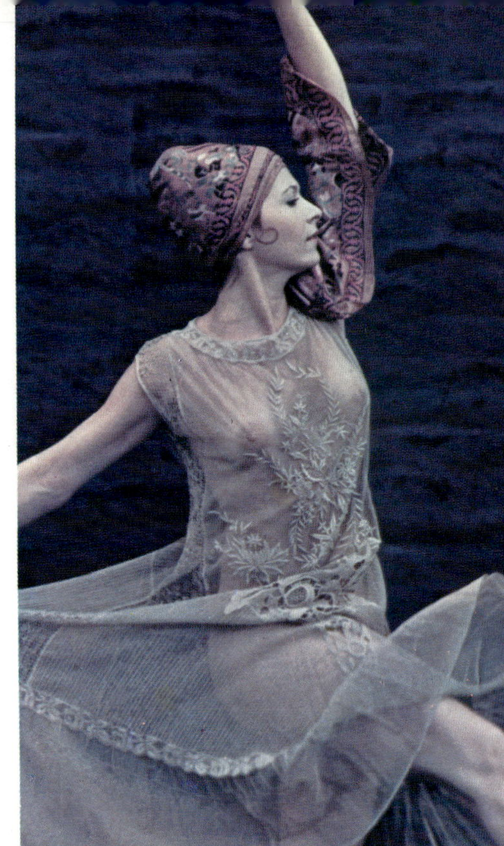

Negative color film

The great advantage of negative color film (p. 23) over positive (reversal) color film (p. 24) is that this material offers the photographer the same virtually unlimited degree of control over the final appearance of his pictures as the black-and-white process. In terms of everyday experience, this means no more worry about over- and underexposure since the exposure latitude of negative color film is as great as that of black-and-white film; hence, no more need for "bracketing" (p. 73). No more worry about shooting in the "wrong" type of light or choice of filter since unsatisfactory overall color can easily be corrected during printing. No more worry about excessive subject contrast since this fault likewise can be corrected in the print through burning in negative areas that are too dense (overexposed) and dodging, *i.e.*, holding back areas that are too thin (underexposed). As a matter of fact, no more worry about unsatisfactory subject coloration since color can be added as well as subtracted while printing "unsatisfactory" color negatives. The accompanying pictures, all of which were made from the same color negative, illustrate the enormous creative potential of this medium.

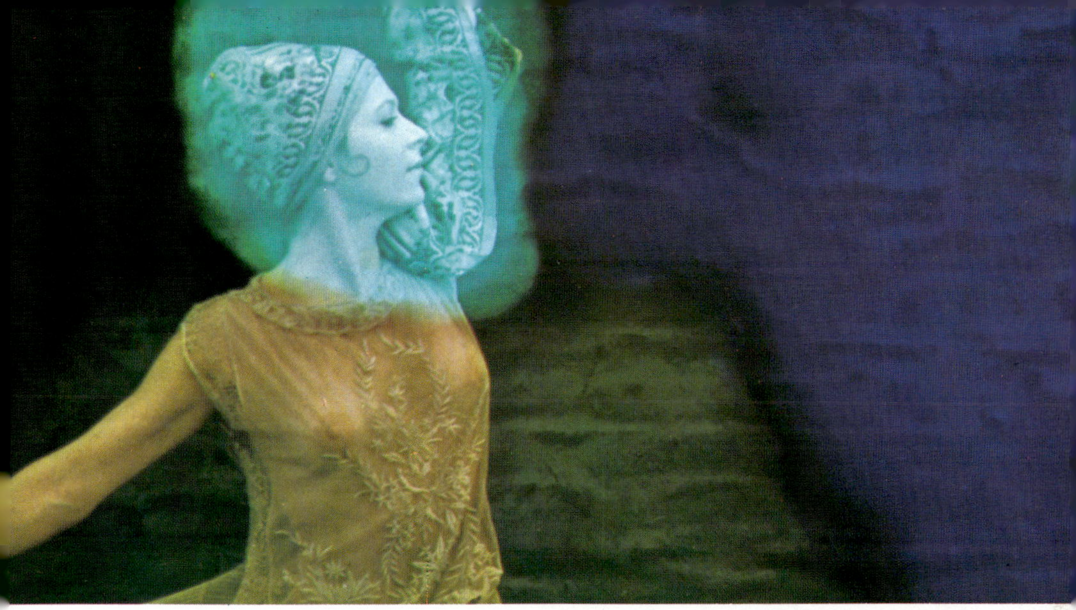

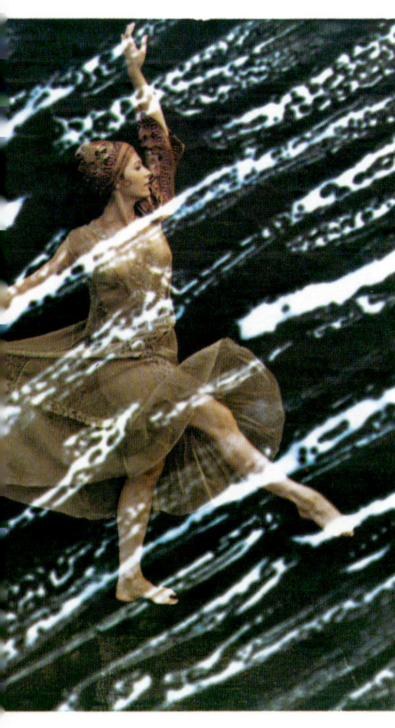

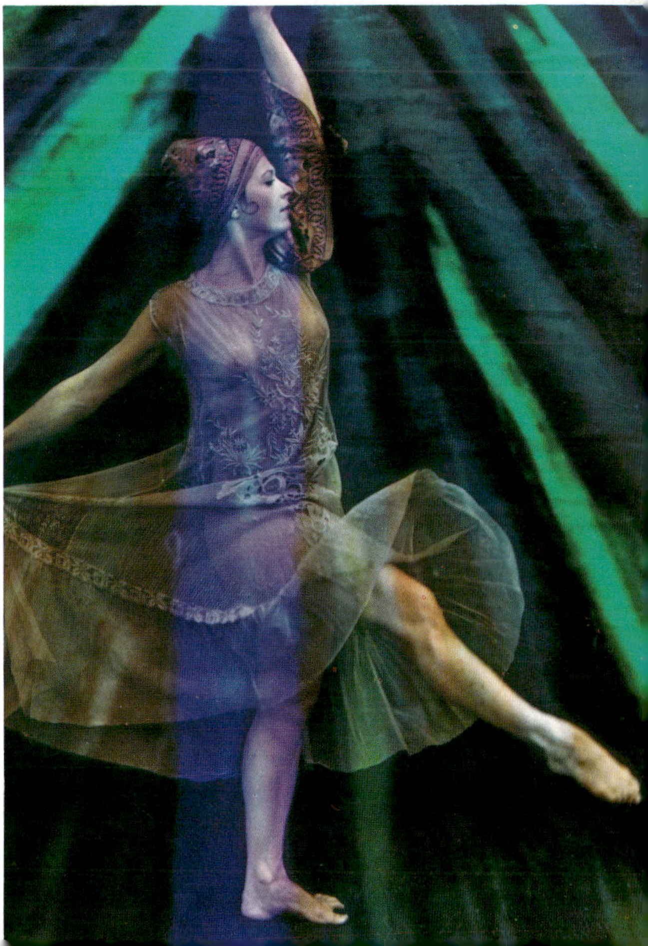

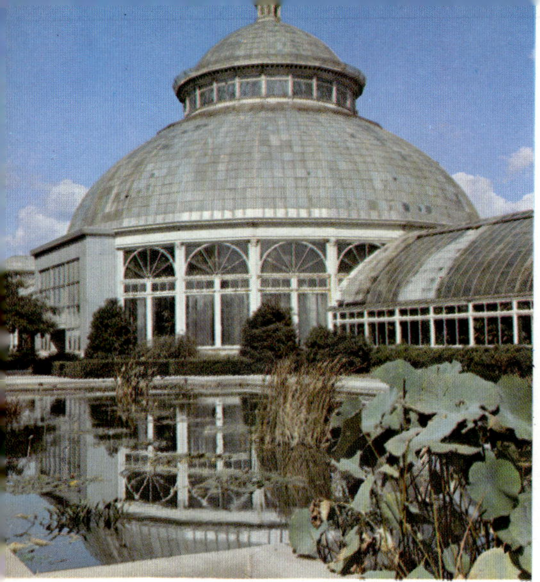

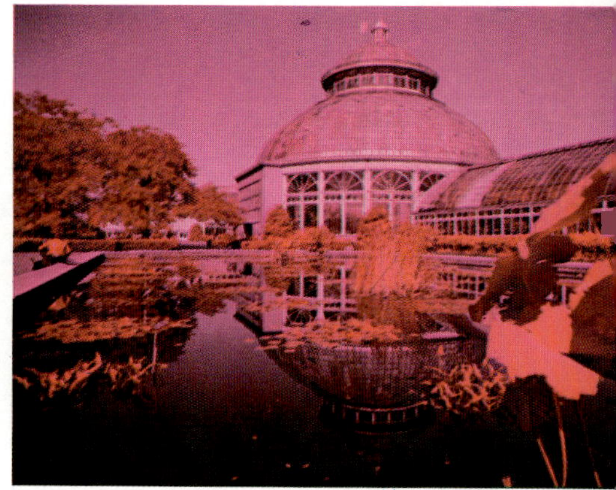

Infrared color film

Experimentally inclined photographers can find opportunities for creating unusual, not to say startling, effects by working with Kodak Ektachrome Infrared Aero 35mm film. This fascinating color material, sensitive not only to visible light (color) but also to certain parts of the invisible infrared spectrum, translates everyday color into rather unpredictable but often beautiful and almost always surprising color effects. Green foliage, for example, is usually rendered bright red, making it look completely "unnatural." But should we reject this kind of rendition merely because we happen to see verdure as green? Or shouldn't we rather use this new means of graphic expression to enrich our experience by creating heretofore impossible effects?

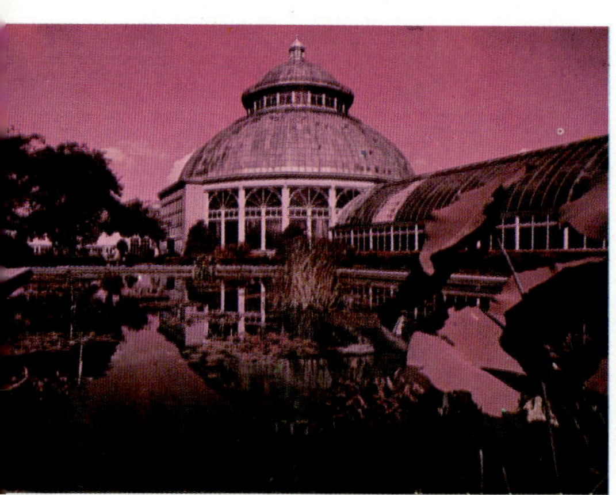

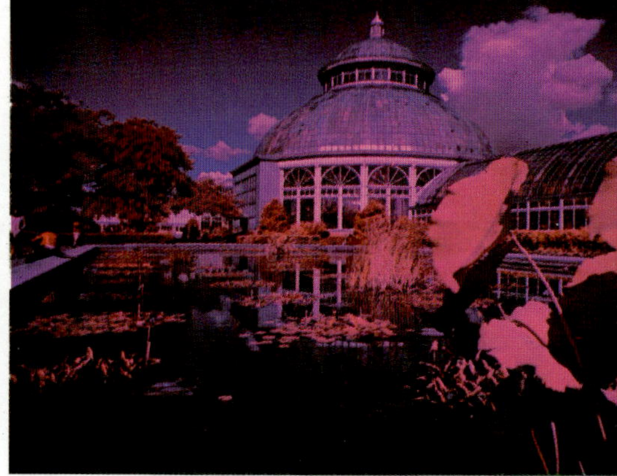

To achieve the typical infrared color effect, the film must be exposed through a yellow or red filter, filters of different densities producing different effects. Average exposure in bright daylight (front light gives the best results) is 1/125 sec. at f/11, which includes the filter factor.

When in doubt, underexposure, because it leads to deeper, more saturated colors, is preferable to overexposure, which produces wishy-washy effects. Bracketing (p. 73) is always recommended.

Since infrared radiation focuses at a point that is somewhat farther away from the film than that for visual light, the lens must be extended forward ever so slightly, preferably in accordance with the red infrared correction mark engraved on many lens mounts.

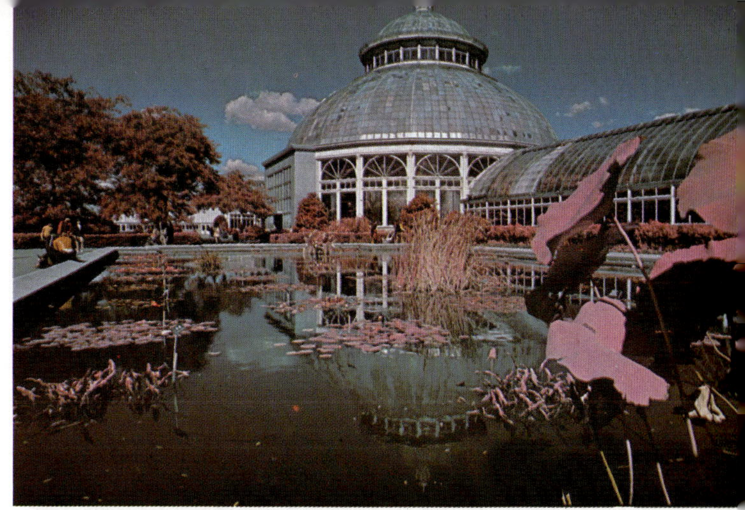

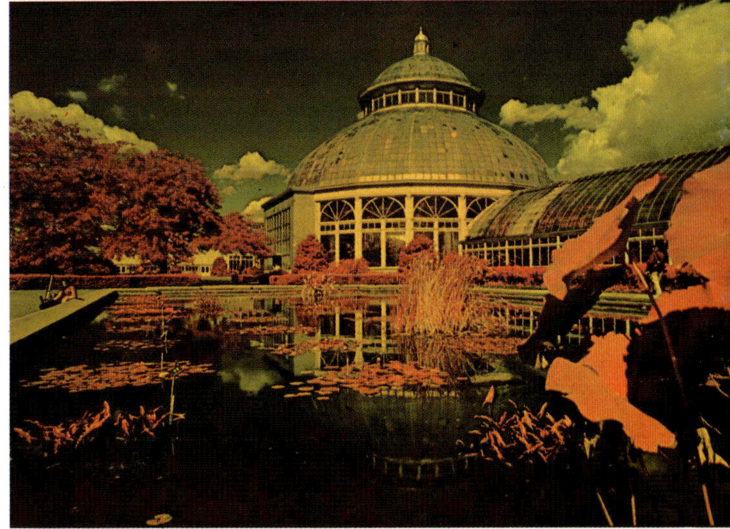

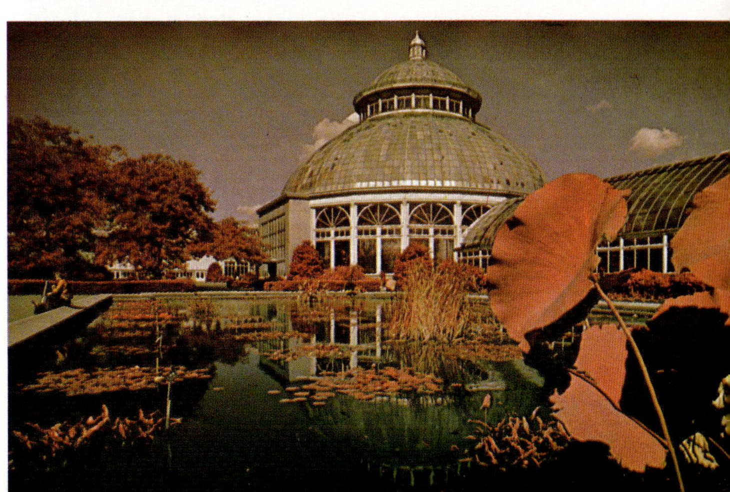

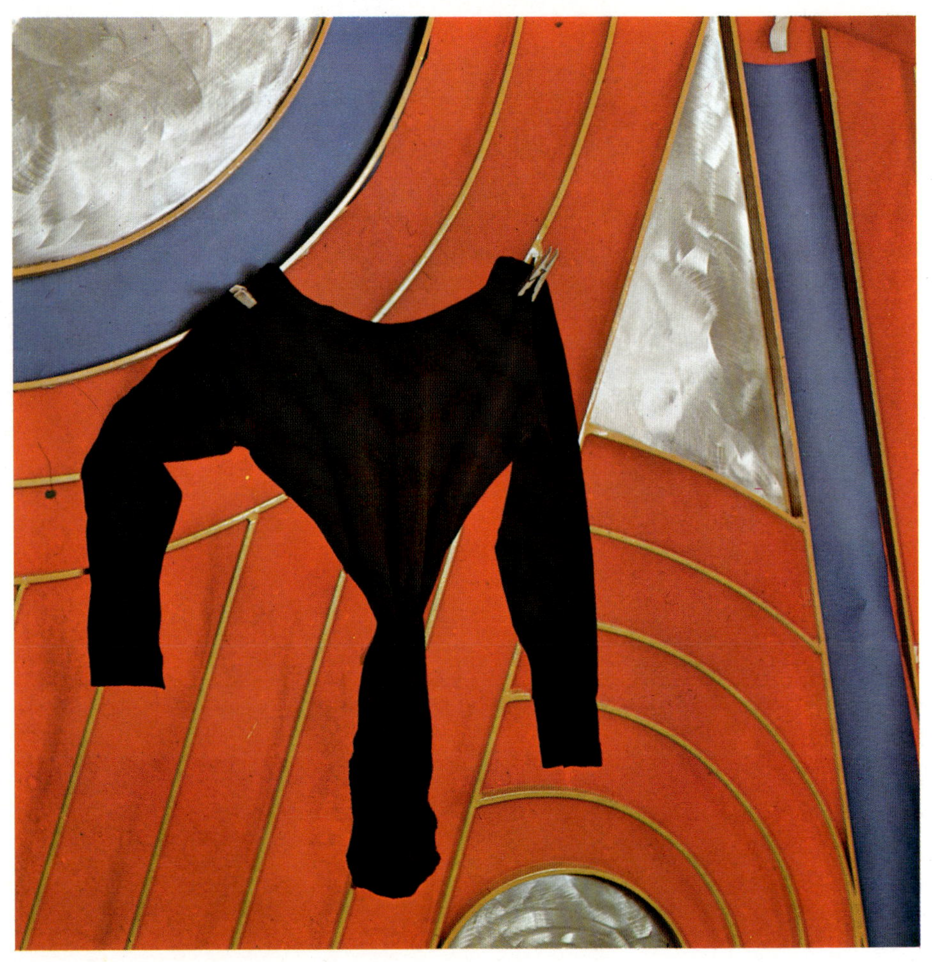

"Abstract" compositions

Creative photographers see and evaluate the subject of their pictures not only in terms of factual reality ("this is a girl, a house, a tree . . .") but also in terms of masses, form, and color ("this is a *blonde* girl in a *yellow* sweater, or a *brunette* in a *red* dress in front of a *blue* door . . ."). And the more they study color and color relationships, the more they develop their sense of composition and become aware of color as a dimension in its own right until, finally, they realize what any artist knows, namely, that an interesting arrangement of color and form is a valid reason for taking a color photograph, regardless of subject matter. This is the moment when they begin to look for "abstractions." The two photographs on this spread show some of the forms such "abstract" color compositions can take.

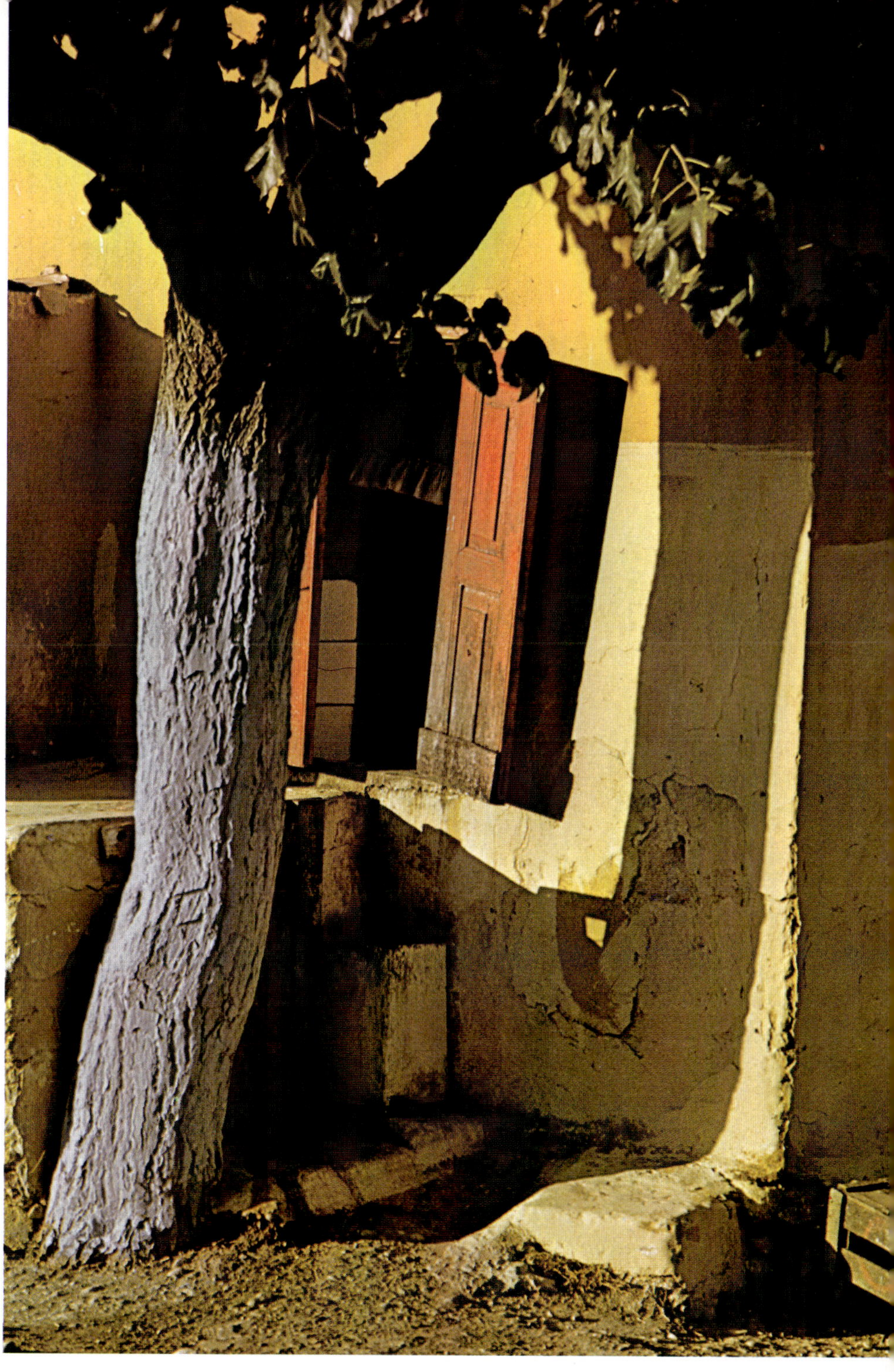

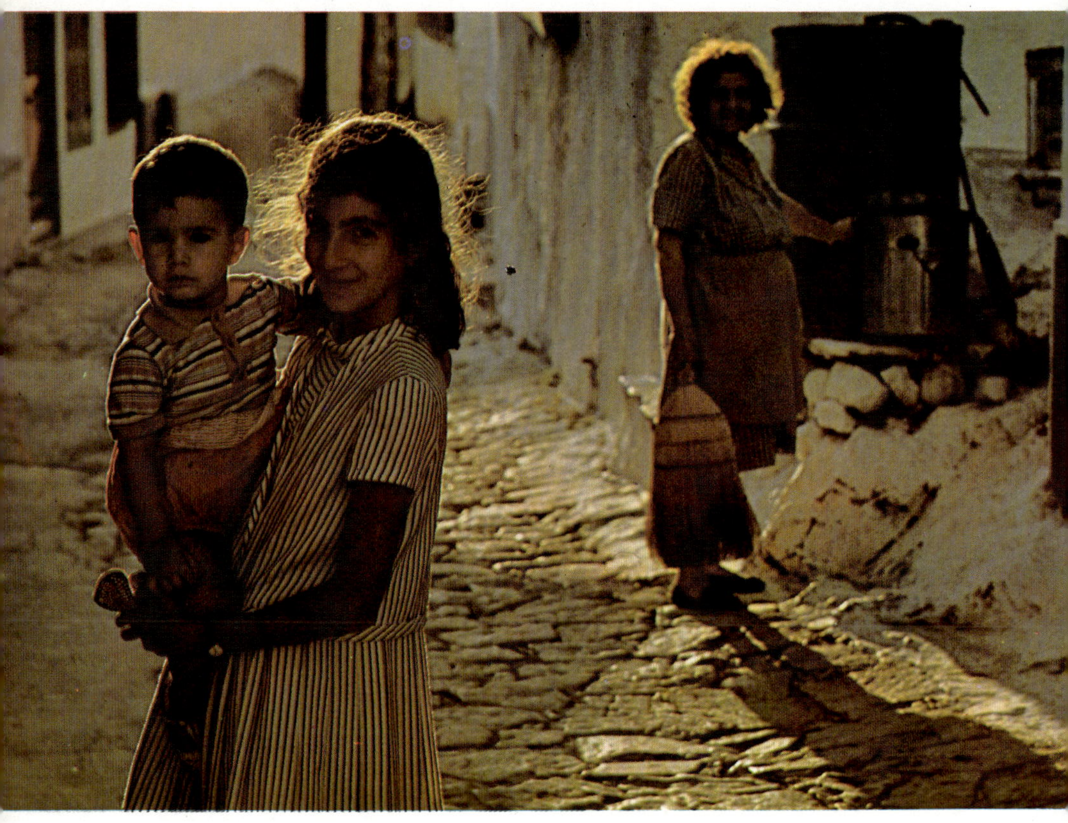

Experimenting with light

Unusual photographs are unquestionably more interesting and memorable than ordinary ones, and unusual photographs are often the result of shooting in unusual light. Creative photographers are aware of this and systematically explore the possibilities of "unusual" types of light: instead of taking every picture in "common" front or sidelight (p. 96), they experiment with backlight (see picture above), trying to familiarize themselves with its peculiarities (pp. 77, 97–99) in order to be able to avoid its pitfalls and take advantage of its creative potential. And unlike the vast majority of amateurs, instead of shooting in "ordinary" sunlight around the middle of the day, they exploit the possibilities of such "unusual" lighting conditions as those that can be found around sunset (opposite page, top) or in the fog (opposite page, bottom).

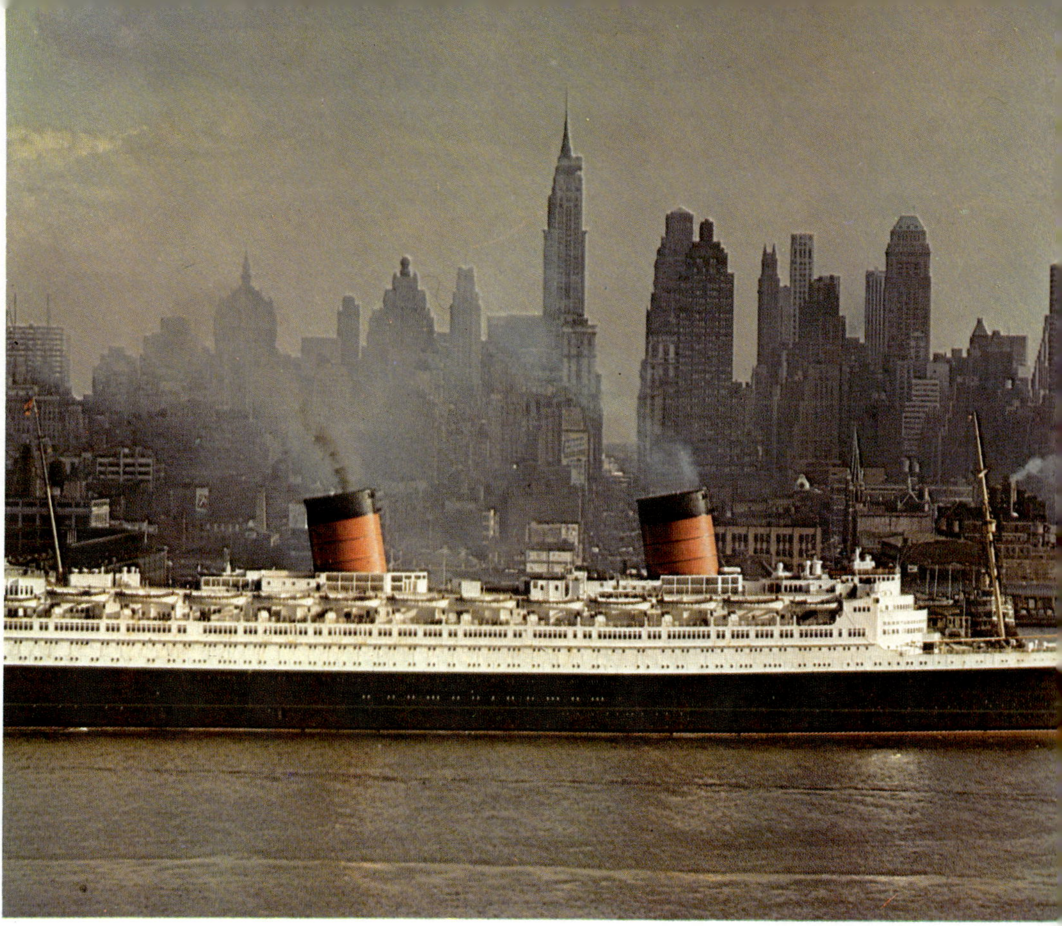

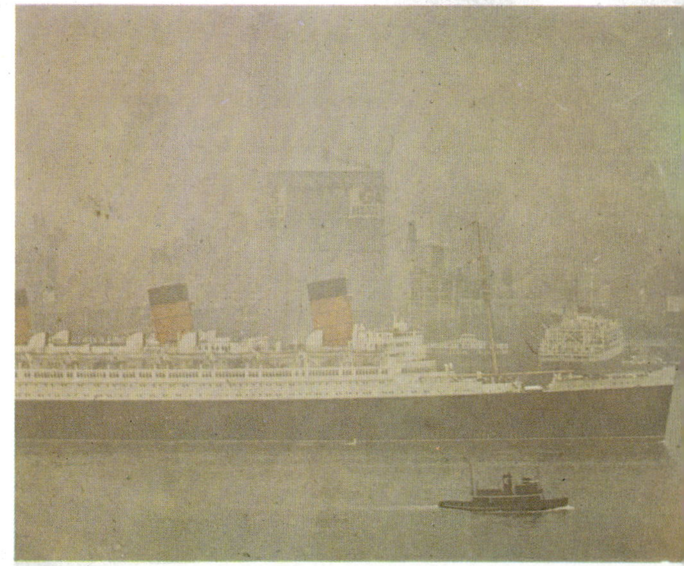

Manhattan across the Hudson. Two photographs by the author—identical subject but different effects, the difference due mainly to the differences in light.

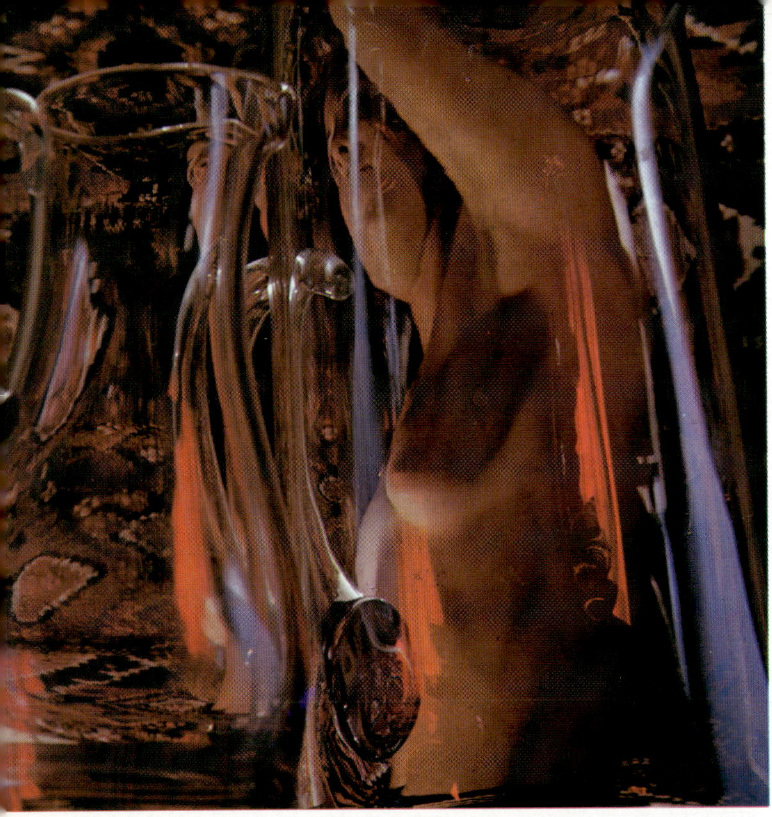

Break the rules

Important as rules are as guides for beginners, they do not necessarily apply to the experienced photographer who knows what he is doing.

Proof of this is provided by the photographs on this spread, which demonstrate some highly effective techniques that violate established academic "rules."

Above: shooting through glass vessels in conjunction with colored light from below creates a mood of fantasy.

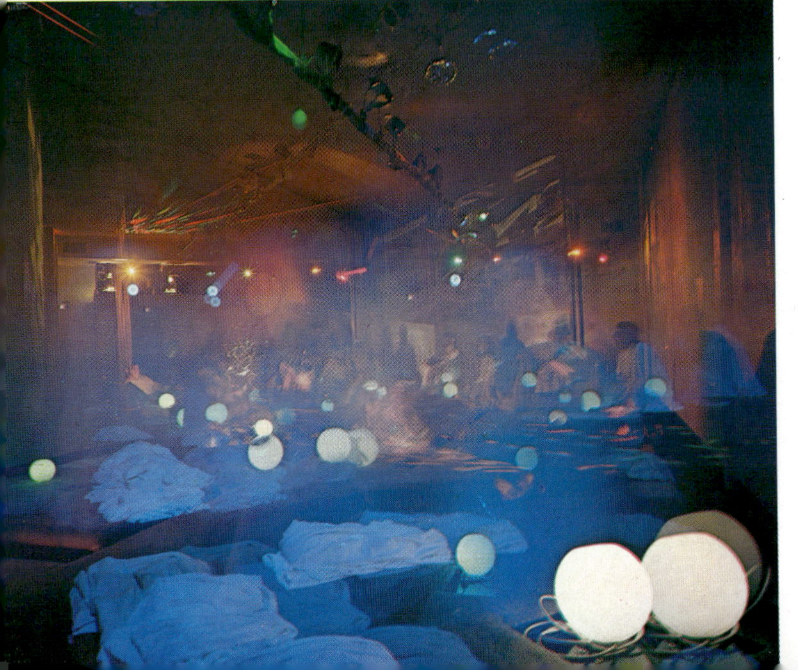

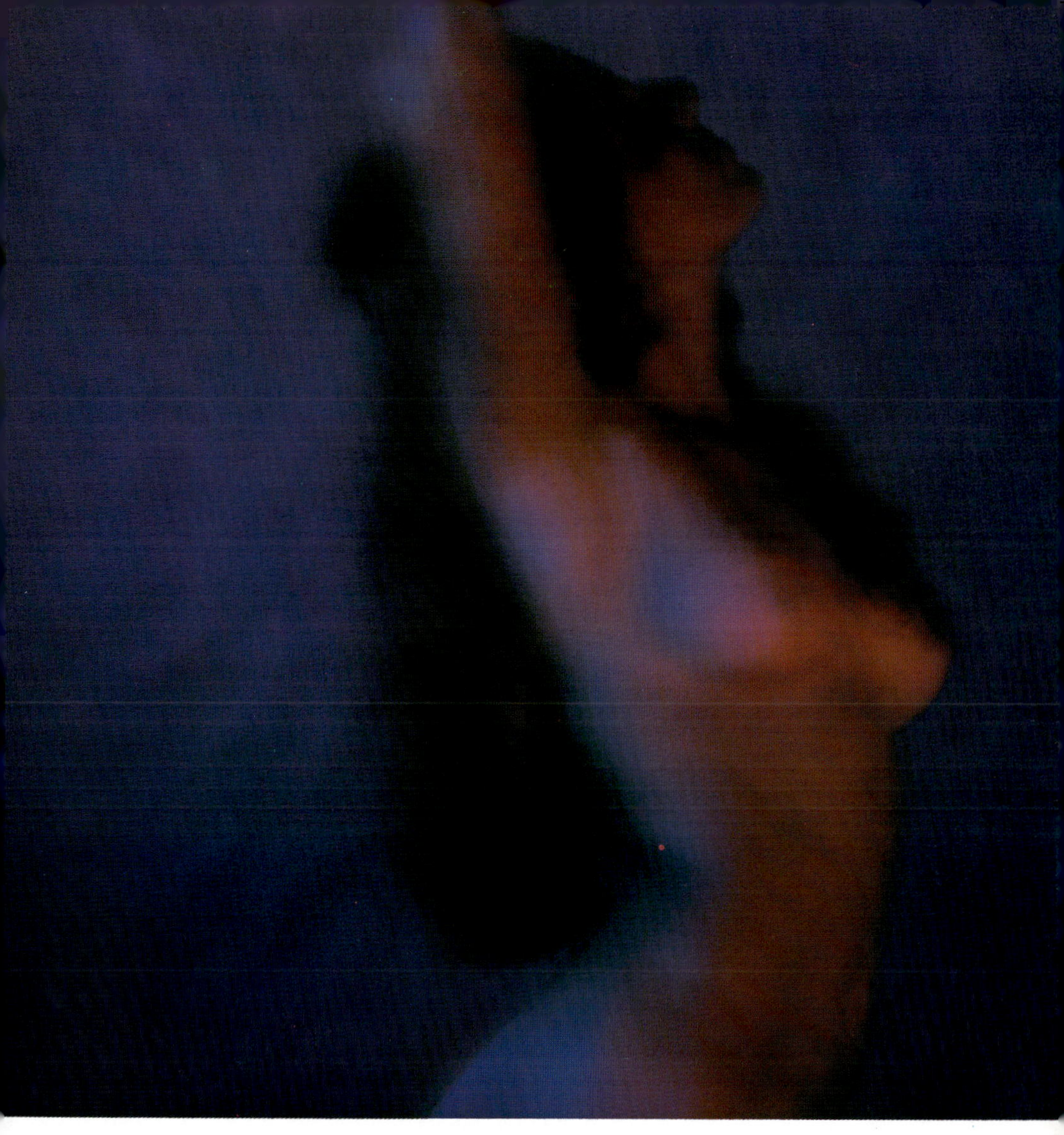

Above: Colored gelatins in front of two photoflood lamps transform an otherwise ordinary nude into a dreamlike vision.

Opposite page, bottom: a combination of double-exposure, deliberate blur through time exposure, and use of colored light effectively recreates the mysterious atmosphere of a psychedelic session.

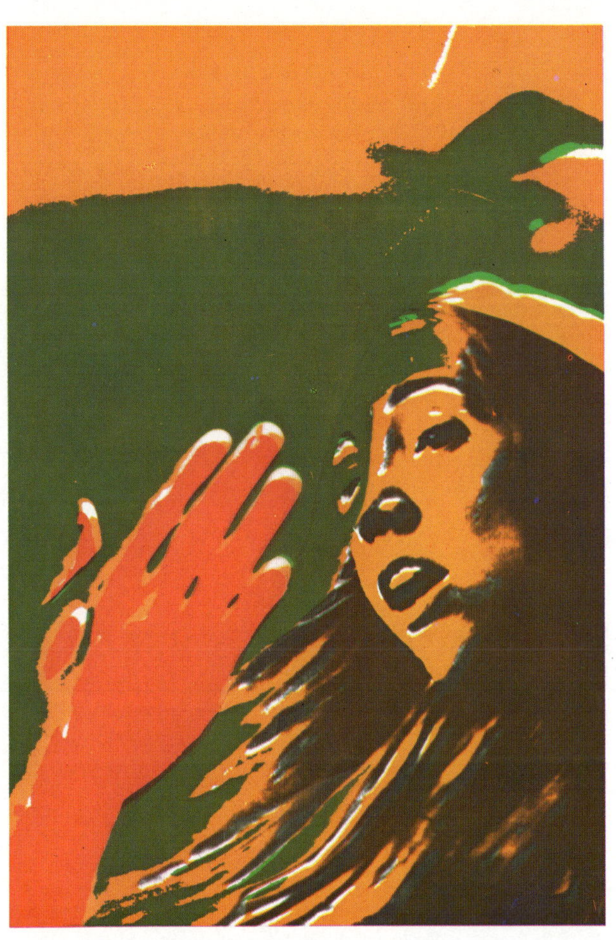

Color posterization

To the imaginative mind, photography provides the means for virtually unlimited creative expression. One of these techniques is color posterization, examples of which are shown on this spread. Although far beyond the scope of this little introduction to color photography, I have included them to give the student photographer an idea of what's in store for him should he decide to go in for, say, advertising photography and poster design (instructions for this technique are given in THE COLOR PHOTO BOOK by this author). Another advanced, highly sophisticated technique is color solarization and still another one, color bas-relief.

These and many others are at the disposal of any photographer who has done his "homework" and familiarized himself with the basic principles of color photography. To help him reach this goal is the purpose of this little guide.

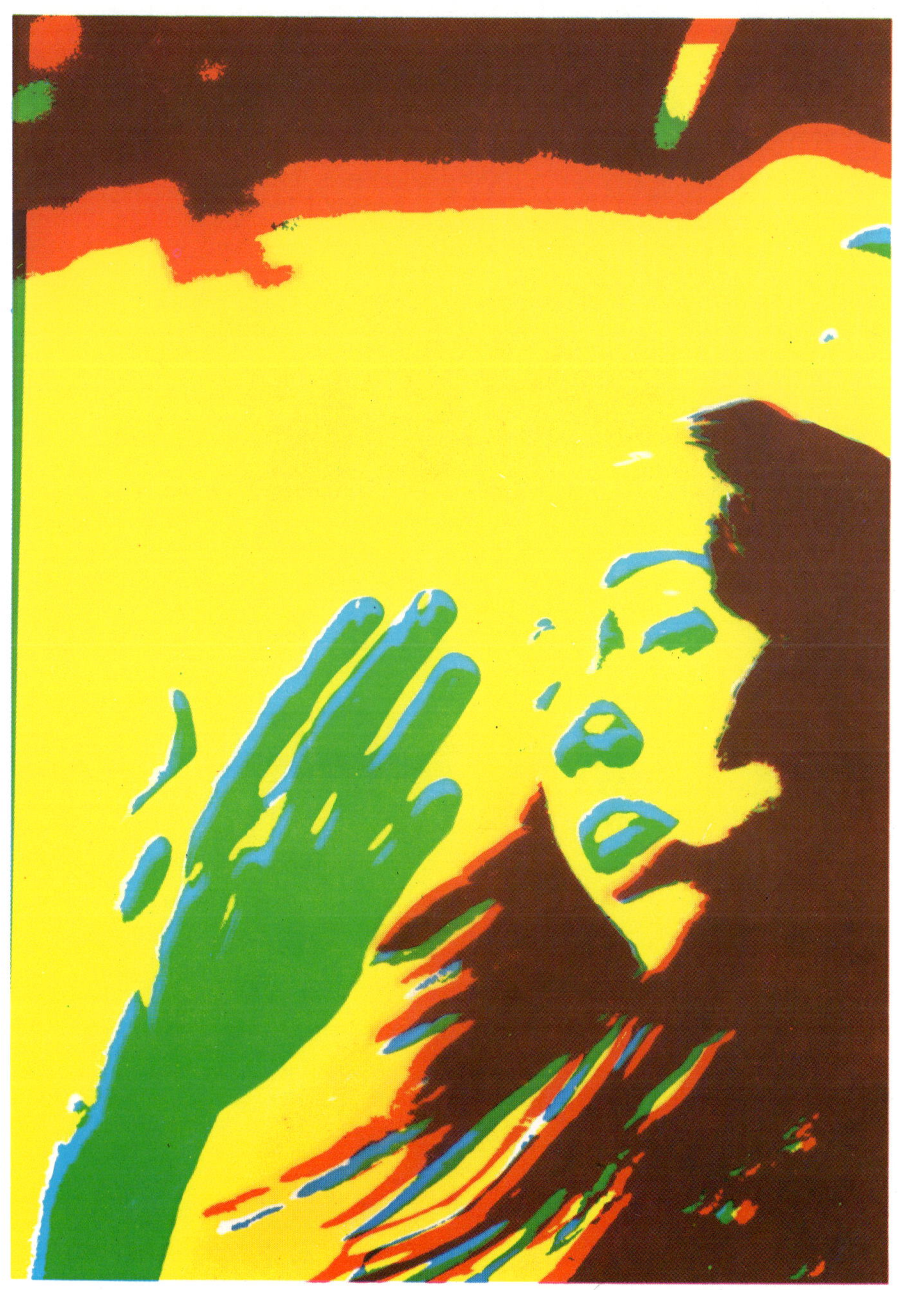

INDEX